sharon hope fabriz

CIRCLING Toward HOME

© 2021 Sharon Hope Fabriz
All rights reserved. No part of this book may be reproduced in any form without permission in writing from the author.

Printed in the USA

11 10 9 8 7 6 5 4 3 2

ISBN: 978-1-7350726-3-0

Cover & Layout Design: Heather Dakota
www.heatherdakota.com

Wyrd & Wyld Publishing
Spokane, WA

Front cover image © Sharon Hope Fabriz
Rainbow image, Adobe Stock © V. Yakobchuk

Learn more at
www.sharonhopefabriz.com

To my many teachers and their geographies

Table of Contents

part one: rally 9

part two: reflect 23

part three: reckon 161

part four: restore 207

epilogue 216

acknowledgments 220

about the author 222

Epistle of HOPE

¹ONCE upon a time there was a traveler who sat on an unfamiliar shore in a driftwood lodge constructed by others long ago, and an eagle spoke another language behind her as quiet water lapped on the sand from the bay. ²The woman gazed up every now and then, letting her pen rest above the paper dappled with rain. ³A dog barked down the beach, and she thought of her own and lurched forward to feel a little closer to home. ⁴She came a long way to settle into the story that had gotten away from her for a while, resolved to get to the truth of the matter. ⁵Was she coming to it now—what she owed herself after years of mapping the valleys and shadows and deaths? ⁶Could she fear no evil long enough to see herself in a full-length mirror, cracks and all? ⁷Could she admit to being the villain and the saint—the genesis and the revelation? ⁸She knew there would be no redemption until she sang true. She had been as duped by the gilded hall of mirrors as the rest of them and for as long. ⁹She left fingerprints where they didn't belong and crashed into walls that crumbled around her in fractals of frustration at the mess she was making. ¹⁰She bent low enough to rake away the broken glass, to sit among the fragments of all that drama. ¹¹Like in a dream, a new design invented itself, one worthy of keeping. ¹²She reflected her wish to be known, her search ending where it began, in stories she slipped under her tongue from her very own yesterdays.

part one: rally

pilgrim path

she wanders deep into the forest,
her wheeled baggage sparking fires.
from the sycamore's crest,
a mute hawk eyes the story
that seethes in her mouth.

she spits at the flames and journeys on
as the forest smolders
with all that needs to be told.

someday, she'll be on a raft in full dark,
coasting trails of wind and water,
wrapped in a blanket of blue,
oars at her feet,
shoes now pillows,
toes dangling in mother sea,
above her star spirals
dancing like sands on tide.

someday she'll swallow that holy communion,
the promise of all that surrounds her.

one

I walked with Mocha under a cloudless California sky, my head wrapped in a red scarf to buffer the November wind. An incoming signal interrupted the voice of a favorite meditation teacher, sending me fumbling for my cell. Some phone calls arrive like flashes of lightning that alter the atmosphere. Mine came from my sister while on this brisk walk with my dog, the walk we take every morning no matter the weather, no matter the day, no matter the errands awaiting.

"Something's happened to Daddy. He can't speak. I'll call you later." The connection ended before I could reply. I pulled Mocha's leash up short, bringing her closer. A gust pushed me off balance. Keep walking, I told myself. Keep walking.

As I approached our front yard, the glory of the golden ginkgo against the cobalt sky fluttered a greeting. "You're beautiful," I said, addressing it as I often did. For an instant, I pinged to the Swedish flag, my family roots, my grandmothers. Then, I stepped through the door and broke the quiet of morning, stunned. "Trish? I need you!"

Soon, in another call from my sister, I discovered that Daddy lay in a St. Paul hospital's emergency center. A stroke? A tumor? An MRI would tell more. Earlier that morning he tried to hang his pajamas on the curtain rod. "Leo, what are you DOING?" his wife sparred.

When he turned toward her, he was all a blather. The look on his face told Jane that things were not right. "Ellie!" she yelled into the hallway. "Ellie!"

My only sibling and younger sister had been in Minnesota for Daddy's latest doctor visit. Ellie was scheduled to head home to Texas the next day.

"Let's go to the car." I could imagine her saying. "We're going to the hospital, Daddy." She must have ferried him down the stairs, their long limbs wrapped around each other in tentative motion. She must have helped him with his coat and explained that she was going to drive. Daddy sat in the front with Ellie, and his wife leaned in from the back. As Ellie drove, she must have taken stock of Daddy's condition. Jane couldn't get her bearings and delivered confusing driving directions. After circling the unfamiliar vicinity of the hospital one too many times, Ellie had the presence of mind to pull over and call 911.

Working toward steadier breaths, I waited in Sacramento by my fully-charged cell to hear what to do next. I fussed over pans of bacon and eggs. My body threw me into control mode. I devoured the protein and encouraged myself to stay the course on my thirty-day purge from gluten, dairy, sugar, and alcohol. Already sixteen days in, I was feeling better for it. Approaching sixty, migraines, muscle aches, and extra pounds weighed me down, but I vowed to give my body a fighting chance to thrive. Anticipating travel, I packed almond butter, apples, protein bars, and herbal tea bags to give myself a decent running start.

Trish, my beloved partner of seventeen years, planted herself out of my way, waiting for a lull in my action. I noticed. Something needed to slow me down. Hot water and lavender might do the trick. "I need a shower," I confessed as I sped toward the tub.

I turned my back on the spray as it pounded my neck. *Keep that headache at bay*, I begged myself, even though the years taught me that I was powerless to stop such arrivals. I angled my head toward my chest, then stretched left and right, groaning at the tightness that reached beyond my shoulder blades. No amount of wondering would tell me what I wanted to know: *What's going on with Daddy?* The scented steam rose like an elixir, and I felt myself soften. Eyes closed, I succumbed to inhales and exhales. "Your breath is always with you," my Tai Chi teacher reminded me more than once.

A voice mail came through when I was in the shower. "Come now. Today if you can." After hearing Ellie's blunt commands, I reserved a seat on a flight leaving that afternoon. I would take the familiar route to St. Paul for the fifth time in ten months, having just returned from Minnesota two short weeks before.

The scent of sandalwood crept in from the living room as sympathetic jazz filled the air. Trish knew how to show care. She caught me off-guard with a hug from behind as I folded warm, clean clothes for the trip. "I'll be here for you, babe. Don't forget that." I turned and held on to her long and hard. A deep sigh finally released.

I texted the kids about Grandpa Leo, then lit a candle and pulled together some words for as much of a prayer as I could muster. *Daddy, feel safe. Rest in a field of love.*

In a moment the world can change. Flashes of bombs or brilliance disintegrate into gristle or glitter and make life something that it hadn't yet been. Civilizations capitalize on it. Economies depend on it. Art expresses it. The dynamism incites what humans call disasters or miracles and what gods call the natural order. I rose that morning to a celebration of sky and leaves more brilliant than any I had seen yet that season. Autumn rustled with its perennial truth. *Life changes when the world is headed toward darkness, and some things put on a show as they go.*

two

My one-way flight had me heading toward mystery. At cruising altitude, the horizon gave way to haze from start to finish. A sudden ticket purchase on the weekend prior to Thanksgiving offered one grace, a window seat.

For months, Daddy had been failing Basic Memory 101. His phone calls came more frequently with the same questions about the same things. No longer was he giving me a list of the latest books he had read, updating me on his jaunts to social functions and cultural events, or outlining the latest honey-do projects on his schedule. His questions shrank to single syllables: *How's school? How are the kids? How old is your car now?*

Daddy's wife, Jane, called both Ellie and me during the previous winter when he was out shoveling snow. She admitted to their troubles and that it was "really getting bad, girls," with the emphasis on "girls." Our appearances in the lives of Daddy and Jane had been limited in the three decades of their marriage, which commenced the year after our parent's divorce. Jane had been widowed several years before. Her daughter Nina was a tad younger than Ellie. We three women had functional relationships stunted by the geographical and cultural formulas that framed us. The intersection where Nina, Ellie, and I met was drawn by blood lines and social contracts, our duties marked by what daughters do—politics, religion, and lifestyles aside.

Daddy's physical presence in my adulthood had been sporadic at best. We all saw each other in spurts, feeling our way on the fringes of each other's lives. Daddy and Jane made infrequent visits to see us, and my trips to Minnesota had been limited to annual long weekends. I couldn't recall ever sharing a heart-to-heart moment with Jane, but the "really getting bad, girls" felt like a cry for help. Even the liberal, lesbian daughter needed to show up.

So it was that I became more actively involved in my father's health. I flew to St. Paul in February, following Ellie's visit a couple weeks before. We were determined to understand for ourselves the scope of Daddy's issues. Our discoveries confirmed the cognitive decline diagnosis, the first stop on the road to full-blown Alzheimer's.

What this suggested was that Ellie and I would be traveling to Minnesota more regularly than we had been and that various tasks would await us: doctor's appointments, senior apartment tours, bank and lawyer meetings—all swirling in the dust storm of what cognitive decline means to the everyday, to the practical, to the future. We would have to prepare alright, although we didn't know for what.

I pressed my forehead against the window, staring onto the desert thousands of feet below. While burrowed into my corner with a book cupped in my hands, I read, and then reread a passage that had the ring of something I learned in childhood. Krishna speaks to his student, Arjuna, in a recap of a a timeless story from a holy text.[1] "Keep all your senses tuned to the ineffable at all times. Listen for and follow my guidance every step of the way." A Bible verse I memorized as a child rose to mind, "Trust in the Lord with all your heart and lean not unto your own understanding. In all your ways, acknowledge Him and He shall direct thy path."[2] The masculine pronouns sidelined me, but the genderless spirit behind them still held power. In an effort to correct the biblical marketing that saturated my youth, and when I had enough selfhood to do so, I composed a new version of that verse that repaired the pitfall of patriarchal pronouns. *Trust in the Source with all your heart and don't believe everything you think*, I translated. *In all ways, acknowledge the sacred, and everything you encounter will instruct your way.* My inability to act as the primary source of my own spiritual life was stunted by nature and nurture, but after decades on the planet, I learned that I could adapt language to fit my experience, my identity, my soul. Why not let those words be with me now to light the path ahead?

[1] Bhagavad Gita
[2] Proverbs 3: 5-6 KJV

A domino of decades dropped me into worlds that insisted I pay attention, learn to ask questions, and decide in all my comings and goings what to take with me and what to leave behind. In my spiritual life, that was most true. How does the child of a lawman and a preacher's daughter end up revising the rulebook of the Judeo-Christian tradition? Let me count the ways.

My hybrid system of spirituality may have insulted purists, but my earthly voyage led me to integrate many wisdom ways. I was wholly responsible for what I believed and how I behaved as a result. I learned the hard way that one requirement for growth involved jumping the white picket fence of my youth, and I banged myself up in the process. This is the story of my journey, one made from strands of time that spun me hither and yon, unraveling my sense of self and my faith in the Almighty. "Turn the wound into light... go into the heart of the difficulty,"[3] I underlined as turbulence shook the airliner.

As the plane descended, the Twin Cities landscape was a lifeless camouflage of browns and grays. Leafless trees rattled a skeleton's welcome, the lakes flat and resigned to the coming ice. When was the last time I had been in Minnesota for Thanksgiving? When I was a child?

Packs of holiday travelers scurried through the airport anticipating turkey dinners and the biggest shopping day of the year. I maneuvered through the crowd and waited in line for a rideshare. My driver was cheerful and talkative, warming up my social skills and letting me release a few jitters as I scoured the scene for some of my favorite views, the neat midwest neighborhoods, the bundled-up cyclists, the quirky storefronts of Dinkytown.

The hospital perched near the banks of the Mississippi River, a reassuring sign. As landmarks went, the river was a hallmark that stretched from my grandparent's past into mine. Daddy's childhood home in South Minneapolis had been less than a mile from the river and even closer to Minnehaha Park

---

[3] Cope, Stephen, *The Great Work of Your Life: A Guide for the Journey of Your True Calling* (2012)

and The Falls, where the creek took its glorious tumble, one I never tired of seeing.

As planned, Ellie met me in the chilly lobby. She commanded a first impression as a substantial, confident woman with a height of nearly six feet. She maintained her self-imposed blond locks in a precise bob. When she saw me, what did she see? Was I the more congenial one? A couple inches shorter than she, my once-highlighted hair had already brightened at the roots to white. Aside from our builds and the number and ages of our children, our similarities waned. Close sisters we were not. We exchanged clever, witty birthdays cards, rarely sentimental ones. Our choices split the sibling bond. I blamed myself and left it at that. Would we ever connect like I had with my closest friends? I hoped that someday we would. I imagined us as two old women sharing a stroll in the park and regretting that we had not tended our sisterhood like we could have.

"Let's sit down." Ellie suggested. We hugged weakly then took the nearest chairs. "The news is not good," she said matter-of-factly. "Daddy has brain cancer. He's got three months, maybe." Ellie was never one to sugarcoat the truth.

I closed my eyes and inhaled. "What! How?" My heart flipped and pounded in a shock of waves. "Oh, no!" I reached out hoping for a hand squeeze but in an awkward motion had to clasp my own hands together instead. Ellie continued in full possession of herself, objective and succinct, like she might do for a family member of one of her patients.

The doctor saw surgery as the most hopeful alternative, and it was scheduled for early the next morning. "I still need to fly home tomorrow," Ellie explained. She supervised a medical team that would be short-staffed and had grandchildren to host for the holiday. "I'll come back later if needed," she assured in a tone tinged with a hint of hope or blind faith that all would be well.

"I'll be in close touch," I assured her. "Is this really happening?" I put my hands to my cheeks.

"It's happening," Ellie said, her eyes tired with sadness and certainty.

In the old days, we would have had a prayer before heading toward the sickbed of a loved one, but these were new days, and we were as different as our mother and father, a split that time tore even further asunder. I wish I would have at least said, "I love you," but I didn't. I dashed to keep up with her as she forged her way down the hall.

three

My suitcase whirred behind me along the waxy floors as Ellie marched ahead. She knew her way around hospitals. My days and weeks on Trish's stem cell transplant floor three years ago stripped me of any desire to visit a hospital again.

Not only that, but even as I planted myself in the forward movement of Ellie's foot falls, my mind sped backward to a younger face of my father, his signature whistle of notes, g-eee-c-g-eee, "Sha-ron, come ho-me." Then memories spilled from the blur of years that held our attempts to manage a connection over differences and distance, troubles and time. Suddenly, everything stopped. Ellie stood waiting at the door.

Entering Daddy's hospital room was like crossing over into a three-dimensional puzzle. My eyes first fell on the family, perched like mourning doves on the long window bench. Jane leaned in the corner, her head tilted against a colorless wall. Had she grown smaller? My definition of her teetered between stepmother and curiosity. She stepped into Daddy's life where Momma left off, in the years when my children were toddlers. As a husband, Daddy had split six decades, nearly thirty years each, between two women with opposing energies and ways. He hadn't spoken to Momma since their divorce.

Jane's only child, Nina, and her husband sat bolt upright, coats stuffed in the space between them. They rose and greeted me with hugs as Ellie reclaimed the tufted chair. My presence completed the family roll call even though I knew the ways I still didn't belong.

I took my place at the patient's side, cold metal rails keeping me at an institutional distance. I held them like crutches, glad for their steely resistance. Daddy was propped at an angle in partial recline, his bare arms dangling from the hospital gown, the likes of which he hadn't worn since his prostate cancer surgery more than a decade ago. Electrodes dotted his head, calculating what they could. He looked like the victim of a Frankenstein scheme, his confused smile and rosy cheeks elevating the effect. I peered into his eyes and wished to crawl inside his mind, to see what he saw, hear what he heard, know what he knew. I had been trying to do that for years and still had few clues about the holdings of his heart. Life long, his affability had been an antidote (a cover?) to untraceable emotions. If I was honest with myself, he and I had that in common.

Over the years, we disrupted each other's lives in our attempts at selfhood, never acknowledging or apologizing for the upsets. Instead, we tromped through them. Daddy gave me a childhood of flux, and I ruffled his conservative feathers. Would we ever come to terms with the righteous indignation we both felt about each other or was I the only one who lived with a resentment that I could not address in any other way but to suppress it? Common courtesy trumped our needs to express ourselves to each other. We maintained a respectable warmth between us that ranked our familial obligations above our opinions about freedom, justice, and love. We each had evidence for our views—the stories of our lives. Still, we upheld certain notions we had been raised to accept, among them that fathers and daughters have duties to each other.

"Hi, Daddy," I said as I placed my hand over his and squeezed. "I'm happy to see you."

His eyes twinkled in what I wanted to be recognition and he nodded. "Dafjcvniresdfa" or something like that ushered forth from him, a new language of crossfires I couldn't translate. Then, he went back to what he had been doing before—pointing to the clock and the white board and to us and back to himself like he was searching for corroboration.

After the exchange at Daddy's bedside, I wedged myself and my belongings between Jane and Nina. I kept my legs uncrossed and tried to lengthen my spine by pushing my palms against my knees and straightening my arms. *Breathe*, I reminded myself. "How are you doing?" I asked Jane as my elbows went slack. I placed my hand lightly on her knee.

"It's been awful," she said. "Did Ellie tell you?" She waved her hand in front of her face and coughed. A word stuck in her throat. "Cancer." She looked toward her husband. She had nothing else to say.

How did we get from a diagnosis of mild cognitive decline based on a brain scan a few months earlier to glioblastoma today? I recalled the neurology appointment three weeks before when Ellie and I waited together in the lobby at the medical center to hear an update on Daddy's condition. He was with the neurologist for a long time before Ellie and I were invited to join in the consultation.

Daddy was nothing if not a master of confidentiality. He made a career of it. "I don't want them to know," I could imagine him saying. Had he received the prognosis? Had he asked the doctors to keep it quiet? Had his smile been his mask or was he clueless to the inevitable? Would the dramatic irony be lost on us? Questions roiled in my belly as my arms squeezed around my middle, my wool scarf a rumpled casualty of my discombobulation.

An hour or so after my arrival, we stood and made the rounds for good night hugs, all of us saving the patient for last. "See you in the morning, Daddy. I love you." I whispered and kissed him on the cheek between electrode pads. "Asdflkjwevfm," he answered, still smiling. Leaving him in a soulless room crowded with a lack of anything that felt like home seemed so cruel. Should I have stayed? Why didn't I even consider it? My regret would boomerang for years.

The hour was late when Jane, Ellie, and I arrived on Moss Road. The house was odorless and toasty, just like Jane liked it. We gave each other space at the coat closet and hung our things in silence. Jane turned to me with a blank stare, "Where will you sleeeeeeep?" she asked, elongating the word into a whine.

"Don't worry about that, Jane. I'll be down here." I pointed to the living room, its miniature settees, its cushioned chairs. Ellie would keep the guest room one more night.

I knew how to be creative. This was a step above camping that I could handle. "Night, ya'll," I yelled up the stairwell prior to shrinking into my own need for silence. I texted Trish a recap of the news so far and promised more tomorrow, thankful that she had the next week off for the holiday. She'd be home with Mocha, and the thought of that gave me peace.

I pulled the settee cushions onto the floor, fashioning a pallet between the wall and the dining room table, then I took the back pillow from Daddy's chair for my head, threw on my night clothes, grabbed an afghan, and set my alarm for an early hour. A dying father on my mind, I searched for a comfortable position and sought a familiar story to settle my soul.

part two: reflect

story seekers

the seeds scatter
in dust and delta,
in blood struggle,
in your own thirst.

gather handfuls
from warriors and sinners,
forage with fugitive angels.

unearth the hollow wreckage,
the bones of belonging.
the relics of loss.

story seekers,
scribe the recollections
mapping the way.

four

"Girls, come up here!" Daddy called from the door leading to the basement. Dutiful, four feet raced up the stairs from Saturday morning cartoons. I edged out Ellie as we burst into the kitchen just missing the coat rack, the grips on our footed pajamas keeping us steady. Ellie toddled to the spot nearest Daddy, and I pulled out a chair opposite, perching on my five-year-old knees.

Daddy moved the bowls of cereal to the sink and unfolded a giant piece of paper full of lines, some wavy like the blonde hair that fell from Ellie's forehead and some pencil-straight and brown like mine. "This is a map," he explained as he flattened the paper onto the slick surface. "I want to show you something." His long frame cast a shadow as Daddy's imposing forefinger gently tapped the top of the paper near a bright yellow dot. "This shows where we are. Minneapolis." He spoke in a near whisper as if he learned the best way to talk to children. "Put your hands on top of mine."

I stretched myself over the table and cupped my hand over Daddy's. Ellie planted her small palm on top. The pale pyramid slid across the map like it was a Ouija board. "We are moving all the way here. To San Antonio." By then, the pyramid had deconstructed itself. His confused daughters scratched their Nordic noggins as Daddy used words like "month" and "movers" and "miles" that we didn't understand.

Arms outstretched, Ellie tumbled into our father's waiting lap.

"How come?" I asked as I brushed away teardrops.

"Daddy's job" was the answer.

"Whyyyyy?" I scampered off the chair and ran to squeeze Daddy's forearm. My whine must have carried, for I heard my mother's uneven footsteps clomping down the hall.

"Leo?" Momma called. "Did you tell them?" Before she could make it to the doorway, Daddy patted me on the shoulder and answered my whine. "Because life isn't fair, Sharon Hope. The sooner you learn that, the better."

Preceding the announcement of the move, Daddy had been absent for many months, away at the F.B.I. Training Academy in Quantico, Virginia. The kitchen table news flash indicated a pattern of future movement. The Federal Bureau of Investigation became a higher power in our family story, playing a decisive role in my fate.

Within months of our arrival in San Antonio and soon after Daddy's thirty-first birthday, the country mourned the death of John F. Kennedy. As a newly sworn F. B. I. Special Agent, Daddy worked on the fringes of the presidential assassination investigation while his young family adapted to life in Texas, a far cry in all ways from Minnesota.

Our family moved onto a treeless street in a new subdivision and attended a small Evangelical Free church that met in what looked like a house. I learned to ride a bike, Momma learned to drive, and Ellie grew from toddler to little girl. Red Skelton and Tom Jones offered weekend entertainment on the TV and life felt safe and simple whether Daddy was around or not. New agents were assigned a first-year office for twelve to eighteen months and then were transferred again. Daddy was no exception. As his rookie designation expired, he received orders for a new assignment six hundred miles east in the Deep South.

During the summer of 1963, six months before the death of President Kennedy, Medger Evers, a Black Mississippian, was assassinated in Jackson just days after he assisted several young Black activists with an attempt to attend the two biggest churches in Jackson, First Baptist and Galloway Methodist. The effort was met with resistance.[4] Ever's murder indicated the racist fervor poisoning the dominant culture populated by White

---

[4] Jones, Robert P., *White Too Long: The Legacy of White Supremacy in American Christianity* (2020)

Christians. Evers had been a central force in disrupting the state's systemic racism, especially around voting rights. The Evers murder followed in a line of murders of Black men in Mississippi including Emmett Till, the 14-year old lynched in 1955. Recorded lynchings over the decades from the 1800s to the 1950s exceeded five hundred in Mississippi alone. Tragically, the local authorities were not reliable defenders of anything but the racist status quo.

What became known as the Freedom Summer of 1964 resulted in a flock of over seven hundred civil rights activists from the northern states joining local Black activists to assist with voter registration efforts and to teach the underserved youth of Mississippi in Freedom Schools on the cusp of long-awaited integration of the state's public education systems.

Despite the orchestration afoot, F.B.I. director J. Edgar Hoover, who did not hide his disdain for the Civil Rights Movement, insisted that the federal government would not give protection to civil rights workers, but that protection would remain "in the hands of local authorities."

That proclamation did not last long. The presence of the outsiders had not been welcomed by White locals, and soon violence answered it. With three civil rights workers missing, suddenly the entire country had its eyes on Mississippi.

The Civil Rights Act[5] was signed into law on July 2, 1964, but in Mississippi, the preceding weeks foreshadowed the impossibility of its implementation in the hot coals of the racist South. The nation's gaze landed on Mississippi soil when concern mounted over the disappearance of the three civil rights workers, two from New York. Under pressure from President Johnson, Hoover, announced the opening of a field office in the last state to receive such a resource. The urgent effort to staff the office would hit close to home. Daddy delivered the news around the kitchen table. We were moving again. Next stop, Jackson, Mississippi.

Daddy reported to his new job on August 4, 1964, the day an informant showed investigators the earthen dam where the bodies of James Chaney,

[5] Civil Rights Act of 1964 banned discrimination based on "race, color, religion, sex or national origin" in employment practices and public accommodations.

Andrew Goodman, and Michael Schwener had been buried. Daddy remembered that detail as a keyhole through which the subsequent years could be seen.

At the end of a long day of unpacking in our new house in north Jackson, Daddy came into the bedroom where Ellie and I were already tucked into our beds. Daddy was taller than most fathers, six feet six inches tall. To say I looked up to him was an understatement. He squatted near me, getting close to eye level, his fresh regulation haircut bringing an unfamiliar harshness to his profile. "Tomorrow we're going to practice walking to school again." he said. "You're almost a first grader, Sharon." He stated it as an accomplishment, so I smiled.

The school was so close we could almost see it through the pines in our backyard, and opening day drew near. The way Daddy told it, Momma would watch from the window as I walked up the hill with the rest of the children from our street.

I took his hand and my small fingers started fumbling with his massive palm. "But what if I can't find my teacher?" I asked, revealing a fear that had been building ever since Momma and I picked out a red plaid satchel from the Sears catalog. My tummy gurgled, leaving a sour taste in my mouth.

"All the grown-ups will be there to help you, and you're a smart girl. I would be there if I could, but I can't. My job is to make sure children in another school are safe. We want them to be safe, don't we?" He stood up, suggesting my answer. "Don't forget to say your prayers, girls." He reached to the twin bed next to mine and gave Ellie a kiss on the forehead. "Nightie-nite," he said as he turned out the light.

I wanted to creep down the hall, sneak near enough to the living room to hear the grown-up conversation between Daddy and Momma. Instead, I slipped onto the floor as I had been taught and folded my hands under my chin. "Please let me find my teacher," I eeked out, "in Jesus name, amen." And with that, I hopped back on the bed and pulled the covers over my head with one question burning in my mind: *Why did other children need MY daddy to keep them safe?*

What could Daddy have been thinking as he walked away from us that night? His oldest was to begin first grade the very year that Mississippi's slow roll toward integration was set to begin—with six year olds. Had he calculated the meaning of the Confederate symbol emblazoned on the state flag? Was he concerned at the national ranking of a Mississippi education, near the bottom of the fifty states? Did he wonder how Mississippi would mold his girls? Did he imagine its power?

The federal government stretched its broad reach into the business of schools with the 1954 Supreme Court decision of Brown vs. Board of Education, which established that racial segregation in public schools was unconstitutional. That mandate had been ignored in Mississippi for ten long years. To the Whites, the discovery of the lifeless bodies of Chaney, Goodman, and Schwerner paled in comparison to the federal push for school integration.

The state's nominal efforts toward ending segregation included a freedom-of-choice method, which put Black parents in the position of registering their children in White schools for integration to succeed. This injudicious response required Black citizens to assume primary responsibility for desegregation with little or no oversight by White authorities. Intimidation tactics involved a full spectrum of violent acts, from verbal threats to drive-by shootings, all meant to forestall the gov'ments intentions.

As an eyewitness to the integration of schools, Winson Hudson, a local Black community-builder and activist, explained that in the town of Carthage, an hour from Jackson, "the last few days before school opened White people were riding by day and night, threatening everyone...."[6] Of the families in Carthage who volunteered to register their children, all but one withdrew from the effort after threats and harassment.

The daughter of A. J. and Minnie Lewis was one child who would rise to the ominous occasion of entering a White school in Carthage on opening day. Little Debra would have a welcoming party of overwhelming proportions: police, marshalls, attorneys from the Justice Department, and one F.B.I. agent. Daddy.

---

[6] Hudson, Winson and Constance Curry, *Mississippi Harmony: Memoirs of a Freedom Fighter* (2002)

Just as Momma and Daddy planned, I joined the neighborhood children for the walk up the hill on the first day of school. We passed a fire truck, ambulance, and several police cars without as much as a hiccup. The city of Jackson was taking no chances on a day like today. Daddy hadn't warned me about the appearance of emergency vehicles, but I took cues from the other children and kept walking toward the front door where a crowd huddled before the morning bell.

My teacher was outside the first grade classroom door to welcome me as Daddy promised. I arrived home that afternoon proud that I was an official school girl and had no imagination for the fact that other children and their families had and would endure hardships for walking into a schoolhouse. In Carthage, part of Daddy's territory, the Lewis family was one of those families. A historical Black newspaper up East, *The New Pittsburg Courier*, picked up the story and reported the following on September 12, 1964:

> CARTHAGE, Miss. – A Negro father kept his promise to the slain Mississippi field secretary for the National Association for the Advancement of Colored people—Medgar Evers—and was fired from his job for doing so. A. J. Lewis, who enrolled his young daughter in the first grade of the Leake County School here Tuesday, Sept. 1, has been notified by the lumber company at which he was employed that he no longer has a job. The daughter, Debra, was the only one of nine Negro children eligible to attend the school under a Federal court order won by the NAACP. Parents of the others bowed to intimidating pressures, levied by white businessmen the day before, and kept their children home.

These details were unknown to me until I researched them myself well into my adulthood. As a six-year-old, the scariest things in my life were the ghost stories that the older kids on the block told on rainy days when we would make forts under folding patio chairs. The monsters of prejudice and hate existed on the invisible sidelines of my life, as cases in my father's F.B.I. files, in the secret plans hatched in Ku Klux Klan meetings, and in the biggest accomplice to the rebirth of the Confederacy, Jim Crow. I didn't have a clue.

Debra Lewis, the first grader who single-handedly integrated Carthage Elementary School, would not live to see the continued horrors committed by the very institutions that were constructed to protect and defend her and all citizens of the republic. She wouldn't live to learn of the perpetual violence, murders of Black men and women, names too numerous to list here, dead by the hands of White terrorists and law enforcement, many shot in the back. Debra died on February 4, 2001, at age forty-three. Rest in power, Debra Lewis, as one of the unsung heroes of the unending march toward freedom.

five

In the middle of my second-grade year, after eighteen months in Jackson, Daddy announced around the kitchen table that he received another transfer. I shot a glance at Momma and my belly went squishy. What about school? I wondered. I loved my teacher, who put me in the blue bird reading group, two levels up from the lowly canaries. I liked the fancy Baptist church we attended with its giant steeple and carpeted sanctuary. Ellie's Sunday School teacher was the daughter of Ross Barnett, the governor of the state. The only misfortune I suffered was that the creamy-skinned mothers of the other Brownies in my troop suggested that Momma put me on a diet, which she did. I had a thicker middle than my rail-thin peers. My allotment of treats at church and at Brownie's was cut in half. All the girls knew that "Sharon only gets ONE cookie" and took to announcing it whenever they could. I was ashamed.

The move to Clarksdale would take us a hundred-fifty miles north. "I hear it's flat as a pool table," Daddy told us. We would depart at the beginning of winter vacation for Coahoma County. The Mississippi River formed the county's western border, and the delta created there had been fed and flattened before the time of Jesus.

In 1830, the Treaty of Dancing Rabbit Creek removed the Chickasaw and Choctaw from the rich farmland of northern Mississippi. Shortly after, cotton production proliferated, and by 1860, Mississippi produced more cotton than any other state. Cotton didn't pick itself. Coahoma County's 1860 census[7] reported a population of 1,521 Whites and 5,085 enslaved people, numbers accentuating the free labor underpinning its profitable agricultural

---

[7] Nearly 150 years later, USDA census data (2017) reported 348 total farm producers in the county, 314 White and 34 Black. In a county where Blacks made up 77% of the population, eighty-nine percent of farms were White-owned.

economy. With the advent of Reconstruction, sharecropping kept the Black community chained to the economics of White power. The culture of oppression inspired art born of injustice. A genre of music fertilized by enslavement and a spiritual relationship with suffering emerged. Clarksdale, the Coahoma County Seat, earned its label, the Birthplace of the Blues.

After the gloomy news of the next transfer, scheduled smack in the middle of my second-grade year, Momma found her most hopeful voice, her most trustworthy tone, and promised that we would be fine. "You'll do just what I did when I was a girl like you. Make new friends! Remember how it goes?" Momma spoke from the comfort of her rocker.

I knew the formula. She had been over it with me many times. Dutiful daughter that I was, I answered from a dramatic standing position, extending my hand for an earnest handshake. "Hi. I'm Sharon. What's your name?"

"And then?" Momma's nod rose and fell in a growing crescendo, encouraging me to speak.

"I ask them what kinds of games they like to play or if they have any brothers or sisters or when their birthday is?" I ended on a lilt in hopes that Momma would signal success with one final nod.

"Good girl. See, you're ready for anything!" She gave me the dimpled smile that assured me she was right. I trusted Momma more than myself. "Remember what the Bible says," she'd add. *"His eye is on the sparrow so I know He watches over me."*

I gave her a closed-mouth grin and leaned down for a hug. "I'm scared." I whispered.

"Of course you are," she said, like it was the most normal thing in the world, and hugged me back. "It's natural to have butterflies in your stomach, Sharon Hope."

Momma wore a leg brace that attached to a clunky, black lace-up shoe, not the fashionable heels that other mothers wore, her smile always won the day. Whenever my cheerfulness flopped, Momma challenged me to "turn that frown upside-down."

"What's that?" a youngster who stood near us in the grocery line or at a church event might ask, pointing to the two thick metal bars growing up from the sides of her shoes and buckled by a thick black strap below her knee.

Patient as ever, Momma would explain time after time that she had a disease that weakened her muscles, that her leg needed more support, that the brace was a tool that helped her to walk. I watched these interactions with pride that Momma could say just enough to help a little child understand and not too much to confuse them.

Momma had only been a child herself when the neuromuscular disease took hold, malforming her feet and requiring multiple surgeries that kept her out of school for months and years at a time. Her stories of living in the hospital, cared for by nuns with only occasional visits from her family allowed, put me on notice that things could be worse for me. Moving wasn't as bad as that. I had no right to complain.

When I was older and more curious, I asked her questions about how she learned that she was *crippled*, as she used to say.

"I'll never forget the day I watched my family walk away from my wheelchair to the sandy shores of Lake Michigan," Momma told me. "I was between surgeries that summer, and I was twelve. The doctor explained what was happening to me, and I understood in that moment that my life would be different than what I expected."

I let those words sink in, feeling a kinship that I couldn't explain. She kept talking, like she was preaching to me. "I watched my parents and my brother jumping in the waves and decided right there and then to live the life that I'd been given." She explained that she didn't want to be angry. She didn't want to be bitter. What she wanted was to be pleasing to God, her smile an emblem of her intentions.

To encourage a productive social life in Clarksdale beyond church and school, my parents involved me in a Brownie troop as soon as they settled us in our new house. New faces surrounded me on all sides. I arrived at my first meeting with the established troop speaking Minnesota's version of English, with its big, round Scandinavian sounds. I wore the same paper-bag-brown uniform as the rest of the troop, but differences would define me as an outsider as soon as I opened my mouth.

The diphthongs of my youthful speech spun the girls into a frenzy. The loosening of adult supervision transformed their public Southern charm to a riot of chants and taunts. "Say *ah*! Say *ah*!" the girls squealed while bobbing up and down on their tiptoes, ground squirrels all. What they wanted was for me to speak a pronoun: the first person singular. As soon as I figured that out, I complied.

"*I_EE*," I shouted in two syllables, wide-eyed, hoping the louder I was, the less they would taunt me.

That just egged them on. "Now say *hah*! Say *hah*!" One of the cute ones was tugging at my sash.

"*HI_EE*," I replied, compliant but shrinking.

"Say it again! Again!" they squawked like magpies.

Within weeks if not days, I was saying *Ah* with the best of them, and *y'awwwl*, too, for that matter. And what I adopted, *Ah* learned to love. *Mah* accent and all the Mississippi-speak that came with it rooted in me. To this day, I don't feel fully myself unless I can loosen my jaw for deltified vowels and airy yowls. I have suffered the bias of having a Southern drawl, tagged as ignorant, unsophisticated, and untrustworthy. But, damn it all to hell, my accent is a tickle of a treasure that lives in these here bones.

My parents never did adopt a twang. Momma just couldn't make her Swedish tongue do what Southern-speak required and continued to bring what others accepted as an undefinable sophistication to town. Daddy migrated into the idiomatic territory required to have common conversation with the menfolk: *howdy, ya hear, sure 'nuff,* and *I reckon,* to reel off a few. I wonder how much of his assimilation was like mine, born of a need to belong.

One word that was never allowed in our home, but was common in the Magnolia State, was a hateful variation of the word Negro. I don't remember exactly how the rule first arrived, but I imagine that Daddy wrote the word on a piece of paper, called me over to his desk, pointed, asked me to silently read what he had written, took my hand, squeezed it, and said in the commanding tone that invoked unadulterated attention, "You may never, ever say this word. It's a dirty word that you may never write or speak." I would have nodded, obedient and glad to have received such clear instructions. I liked knowing exactly what I should and shouldn't do.

When that word erupted on the playground or in heated conversations, I never failed to announce the order I had been given: "My daddy doesn't let me say that word." As I matured, I understood the harmful intentions of the word for myself and didn't need to fall back on my father's command, but as a child "Daddy doesn't let me" was a failsafe version of what my peers called wimping out and I called being a good girl.

I was grateful for his counsel but wish Daddy would have given me the history lesson to explain why such a word existed in the first place. He was full of general declarations. "Just because." I wish I had known to ask him to be more specific, but instead I mirrored him with general compliance. Other agents had crosses burned in their front yards, and Daddy, I learned later, had been spit on and cursed at more than once for being a Fed. Was he distancing me from the specifics for my own good? Had it never occurred to him to explain to me what all the trouble was about? Or did he ascribe to the fairy tale that ignorance is bliss?

My days were full of the goodness of neighborhood friends and kind teachers and blocks and blocks of quiet streets where crime was an absent character. Daddy didn't speak of his work except for the occasional far-fetched dinner time stories he told as morality tales. His cases were mostly confidential, so his work life became confidential, too. Momma claimed that the F.B.I. turned Daddy into a cynical man, and she may have been right. He was committed to the letter of the law and was wary of anything that endangered that. The continued violations of civil rights mattered to him strictly in that regard. He kept quiet about the related violence. During those years, the crucifixion of Jesus was the bloodiest act I encountered and that, I learned, had a happy ending. My blinders were secure. I didn't even know to feel for them. Until I did.

My childhood as a transplant to Mississippi's world of Whiteness was fashioned by Southern charm, a trick of eye. The Magnolia State seduced me, uninformed child that I was, into loving its segregated church socials, segregated movie theaters, segregated restaurants, segregated Halloween carnivals, segregated bowling alleys, its segregated Girl Scout troops, segregated libraries, and its segregated schools. The South was all ruffles, blue jeans, and sweet tea, and kept its confederate secrets to itself. My ignorance kept me indifferent, and the church kept me busy. Years later, I learned that I lived alongside injustice, untouched, advantaged, and duped by it.

On weeknights, as Momma sat glued to the image of Walter Cronkite on the national TV news, I adopted the habit of pacing. I worried Daddy home with my waiting by the window and appealed to the God of Matthew, Mark, Luke, and John to keep him safe. On most nights, the lights would eventually flash against the living room mirror, and the slam of a car door would have me scuttling into my bedroom.

"He-LO-OH!" Daddy shouted in tempo with the steps of his size 13 shoes and the slap of the screen door. He went straight to disarm himself of the tools of his trade and placed his gun, credentials, and sunglasses in a still life on his bedroom dresser. I doubt he ever suspected my prayerful efforts for his safe arrival or the tummy aches that caused them. On the nights when he didn't arrive until much later, I was convinced that my faith hadn't measured up to a mustard seed[8] and that his absence was all my fault.

When he did arrive home for our six o'clock dinners, Daddy would drop slivers of stories that were designed either to make us laugh or shiver. One night, he told us how he apprehended a draft dodger[9] hiding in a bathtub behind a shower curtain. On another, he divulged the tale of a suspicious man at a park who was caught offering children candy. Never were the stories about the Ku Klux Klan, whom he surveilled in the middle of the night, or the Black civil rights workers on whom the F.B.I. spied. We all knew he was on the trails of someones or somethings over the course of many early morning departures and missed dinners when he was, in his words, "on a

---

[8] "If ye have faith as a grain of mustard seed, ye shall say unto this mountain, Remove hence to yonder place; and it shall remove; and nothing shall be impossible unto you." Matthew 17:20
[9] During the Vietnam era, approximately 570,000 young men were classified as draft offenders, and approximately 210,000 were formally accused of draft violations; however, only 8,750 were convicted and only 3,250 were jailed.

case." When he was home, Daddy's favorite spot was in his recliner behind the daily editions of the Clarksdale and Memphis newspapers.

After Daddy left for work or was busy with yard chores, I took to scanning the day-old *Commercial Appeal* for headlines, photographs, and answers. The Vietnam War, women's liberation, anti-war protests, civil rights stories, and LSD suicides were all divulged in conservative style. Dr. Martin Luther King's assassination, seventy short miles from Clarksdale, headlined the newspaper's front page on April 5, 1968.[10] I didn't understand everything I read, but in the published photographs of Reverend King's funeral, I saw the pain in Coretta Scott King's face and wondered what it would be like to be one of the children of a man who was killed because he was hated for the color of his skin. Something hollowed in my heart when the adult voices around me fell silent. As far as I understood it, the White community in Clarksdale, my parents included, shed no tears at the loss of Dr. King.

I wondered how Nola felt about Dr. King's death. She was the grandmotherly woman who entered our home weekly to do Momma's ironing, a task made difficult by her disease. I rubbed up against Nola's arm one day as she taught me how to iron a man's shirt. Imagine my shock when her blackness didn't rub off on me as I expected. Momma regularly invited Nola to take lunch at the kitchen table, but she gently refused and went to her car every Thursday at lunchtime to enjoy her sandwich there. She dignified herself within the culture that we still didn't fully understand.

Within days of Dr. King's death, my parents hosted a tenth birthday party for me in my family's small dining room, the first ever with invited friends. I remember the flimsy shorts set I wore: the yellow knit top pimpled with nipples that poked into the fabric like uninvited guests and the splashy floral shorts that stretched at the seams when I sat. A headband pushed back my dull brown mop, accentuating the teeth so ready for the braces Daddy promised. The mirror rejected my Miss America dreams.

---

[10] On April 4, 1968, after delivering a speech in support of the Memphis Sanitation Workers Strike, 39-year-old Martin Luther King, Jr. was assassinated in Memphis, Tennessee.

As we ate cake and ice cream off of Flower Power plates, I covertly checked the expressions of the two most popular girls. Were Sue and Candy having fun? That's the way my tenth year started. With growing worries.

Summer soon arrived and my first-ever week away from home with it. Daddy drove my friend Sue and me to church camp somewhere in the Mississippi thicket. By midweek, I was in over my head, no matter that my counselors were real live teenage girls or that we had arts and crafts, songfests, and campfires with s'mores. None of that mattered in the deep end of the tepid swimming pool that Wednesday afternoon when the promise of Saturday's return home seemed as faint as a July breeze.

My salty sobs mixing with chlorine, I hung on to the pool's edge, praying that no one would notice my shriveling ability to hold myself together. Between gasps and sniffles, I whispered to unmoved water, *I want to go home! I want to go home!* A sloppy version of Dorothy from *The Wizard of Oz* comes to mind.

Soon I heard myself pleading with a stocky blonde lifeguard, who spotted me clutching the pool's hot concrete edge. "Let me call my momma, please! I need to talk to her. Please, please, PLEASE?"

Between my exaggerated gulps for air, she answered. "You're just homesick. Believe me, you'll be okay." Her bare feet slapped away on the sidewalk like a spanking. Was that a no? Couldn't she see I was dying? I hated her. I hated camp. I hated the entire state of Mississippi and maybe even Jesus.

But sure enough, the blazing sun finally set on my red-rimmed eyes. Saturday arrived, and it was time to pack and go. I still had to survive a three-hour ride with Sue, who was gleefully reunited with her parents. I hid my jealousy but could barely stand it when we made a stop to tour a historic antebellum home on the Natchez Trace. The docent pointed out the horsehair bench in the entryway like I would be impressed with such a thing. All I could picture was a dead Black Beauty[11] and my parents very, very far away. No future loneliness ever hurt as much as that first separation when my heart burrowed into a lightless hole. No future return ever comforted me

---

[11] "...people may talk as much as they like about their religion, but if it does not teach them to be good and kind to man and beast, it is all a sham..." Anne Sewell's *Black Beauty*, Chapter 13 (1877).

more than when my heart burst into full sun at the sight of home.

"That's Daddy's gun." I pointed as I leaned near the edge of the tall dresser in my parent's bedroom. The pistol, polished to a high gloss, sat beside Daddy's official credentials, concrete indications of the lawman who lived there.

The lawnmower groaned as it would on any given summer Saturday. Joined with the window unit air conditioner and nearby electric dryer, the conveniences sounded like the soundtrack from a war movie. I didn't have to whisper but did have to keep my eye on Daddy as he crisscrossed the front yard like a soldier preceded by his machine. Momma must have been on a weekend errand with Ellie.

"We can't touch it!" I demanded of my most worldly friend, the one I had to impress with more than my book collection and the Top 40 tunes I learned to play on the piano.

Candy was on the top rung of a loose band of neighborhood girls who rotated best friends in a cycle that always seemed to leave someone out. She was a prime bestie catch who attended not the Baptist church like the rest of us but a more secular one, which my parents looked upon with suspicion. And she had a pink princess telephone of her very own.

"What's it like having a G-man[12] for a dad?" Candy asked as she raised herself on her tiptoes and touched her finger to the barrel like it was a hot iron.

"Don't!" I squealed and grabbed her elbow. "Stop!"

"Has he ever killed anybody with it?" she asked, coming down on her heels.

"I don't know," I shrugged. To me, the gun was a tool of Daddy's trade. Candy knew it was more.

"Can I ask him?" she pleaded, her overbite lengthening into a wicked smile as she swung her blond ponytail like a whip.

My voice went down two full octaves like Daddy's did when he was

---

[12] American slang for an agent of the Federal Bureau of Investigation

correcting me. "Don't you dare! You'll get me in trouble." I sounded like Marshal Matt Dillon from *Gunsmoke*.

Candy raised her index finger again, and in my effort at compromise, I didn't stop her. She touched the barrel of the weapon longer this time, then put the finger to her mouth and licked it. "It doesn't taste like anything."

The lawnmower sputtered out as its wheels bumped across the driveway. I pulled Candy by her shirt tail. "Come on! Let's play hide and seek." As we sped toward the back door, I wondered—*had* Daddy killed anybody? Why hadn't I ever thought of that?

A new day dawned when I realized that there were questions I hadn't ever thought to ask. Ones that other people were asking! Sudden power inhabited the words *What if, Why,* and *How*. Like magic, questions became balloons, kites, sails, geese, sky things. Upward I sent them, secret prayers from a girl finding a way to make contact with all she didn't know.

six

When I was eleven, and because I knew how to follow directions and please adults, I walked the Baptist church aisle one Sunday morning, professing faith in my Lord and Saviour. This act was the next in my ticket to baptism, a full dunk, not to be confused with the marginal Methodist sprinkle. I had already met with the pastor and repeated a prayer that covered all the doctrinal bases to insure my eternal salvation. I believed with all my heart that I would be "washed in the blood of the Lamb."[13] Myriad hymns I learned over the years assured me with redundant reminders that I was a sinner, unworthy, guilty, lost, and in grave need of a cleansing.

Even "Amazing Grace" in all its melodic glory cornered "a wretch like me." One Sunday afternoon after having sung the classic during the morning service, I swiped one of my favorite books, the paperback thesaurus, from the family bookshelf and turned to the Ws and down to *wretch*. I discovered that each synonym listed was more disturbing than the next: *miserable being, contemptible person, scoundrel, castoff, swine,* and *worm*. Gross! I thought. I was confused that the entire congregation sang the song with such gusto when decked out in their finest, not a swine or worm in sight. I knew we were sinners, evil to the core, but why were we singing this about ourselves?

On the bright Sunday morning when I would join the church, my hair curls were wound extra tight. I wore a white dress with a yellow ribbon at its princess waist, a style that let my thickening thighs float free.

As the third verse of "Just As I Am" began, I rose to my feet. An old man had already walked the aisle, Baptist-speak for answering the altar call. I needed to get down to the front of the church before the song ended. With

---

[13] "Washed in the Blood of the Lamb" American hymn by E. A. Hoffman (1878)

four more verses to go, I would have plenty of time. I left my balcony seat, waved smugly to my friends, and skittered down the red carpeted stairs, feeling my curls and thighs bobbing away.

Momma and Daddy smiled at me from the choir loft as I moved toward the front of the church in practiced Miss America style, like I was balancing a book on my head. My elderly prayer partner from the Missionary Circle stood and gave me a hug as I passed by her pew. "Awwww"s rippled through the air. In front of the congregation, I answered yes to three questions. Do you believe that Jesus Christ died for your sins? "Yes." Do you seek membership in this church? "Yes." Will you support your church with tithes and offerings? "Yes." I didn't know until I got home that Daddy would expect me to take my tithes out of my allowance. That came as a budgetary blow.

I was baptized on a Sunday night several weeks later along with a couple of friends and a line-up of white-robed women and men. We stood in the backstage passage leading to the reservoir called the Baptistry. The blood red velvet curtains that usually concealed the deep tub inset above the choir loft were opened for baptisms. Aquarium glass allowed the congregation to see the new members at full tilt when the preacher dipped each one backwards into the tepid waters far enough for their robes to billow and their heads to rise with wet hair slicked flat against their skulls. Awkward exits were common.

I had been groomed for heaven in all conceivable ways. I was fulfilling the requisite Baptist curriculum by attending Sunday School, Training Union, Girls-in-Action, Youth Choir, Vacation Bible School, and church services, Sunday morning, Sunday night, and Wednesday night, to be exact. That didn't include the weeklong revivals that came around twice each year. The codes of the Baptist faith became as familiar to me as my own face.

Itsy-bitsy was how my friends described my family as they reeled off their extensive lists of uncles, aunts, and cousins. Daddy was an only child, and Momma had one brother with a wife and son, our only cousin. Our grandfathers were long dead. Except for weekly phone calls, handwritten letters, and annual visits, our widowed grandmothers, the family matriarchs, lived only in picture frames on the coffee table. Summer visits to see our grandmothers in Minneapolis and Chicago guaranteed their existence, but Ellie and I didn't have the perk of grandparents nearby like all of our friends did.

To remedy the space between us, Daddy arranged for the grandmothers to visit our Southern homes. The week before their visits, Momma would wear herself out cleaning and refused to let us bathe in the tub once it had been scrubbed for company. When I grew as tall as the broom, which I did by the fourth grade, I was expected to help with the chores: washing dishes, setting the table, vacuuming, dusting, changing our bed sheets, and sweeping the driveway and sidewalk. Daddy's mother, Grandma Sig, took up residence in Clarksdale's downtown hotel for an extended stay each spring. Our house was too small to have a guest for more than a day or two, and Grandma was nothing if not independent, so that suited her just fine.

Upon the occasion of my eleventh birthday and because I had been an obedient girl, Grandma arranged a rollaway bed in her room at the Regency Hotel and invited me for some special time with her alone. We would see a grown-up film, a famous one that she assured me I would love. Momma wasn't a fan of the theater, holding to the conservative taboos[14] of her upbringing. No telling what amount of negotiation it took for her to agree to Grandma Sig's plan.

Grandma Sig was the kind of woman who painted her nails and wore Estee Lauder's Youth Dew perfume and had more shoes than our whole family of four put together. She worked at a bank in the real world and didn't talk about Jesus all the time. She played the piano by ear, sang Broadway tunes, laughed at my jokes, and cooked up the best Swedish meals I had ever tasted. She had been a single woman for as long as I could remember, and I adored her personality, her independence, and her story of survival after being orphaned at fourteen.

I stood under the marquis at the theater as Grandma, decked out in a bell-bottomed pants suit of bold orange and brown swirls with clunky gold jewelry and shoes to match, explained that the movie we were going to see

---

[14] In addition to condemning alcohol, many strict 20th century Baptists also decried card playing, gambling, dancing, and going to the movies.

had been made thirty years before and was on a special anniversary run. "We're so lucky that it came all the way to The Paramount in Clarksdale!" she exclaimed, making it sound like the most important event in the world. She went on to explain that the movie was so long that it would have an intermission. And then she explained what an intermission was.

I examined the movie poster. A dashing moustached man held a raven-haired beauty in his arms while buildings behind them burst into flames. I was afraid the story would be too complicated for me to understand and the passionate embrace scared me a little. My parents didn't hold each other like that. As I grew older, the special memory turned out to be more complicated than I originally feared. As my knowledge of racism grew, so did my shame that I had fallen in love with *Gone With The Wind* as I sat transfixed in the theater, holding my grandmother's hand.

seven

The most stark diversities among the children in my class regarded our height, weight, what our daddies did for a living, and what churches we attended: Methodist, Presbyterian, or Baptist. Anything else was simply heathen,[15] Catholics included. Jews were a separate category altogether, confusing me no end. I learned from Sunday School that Jews were God's chosen people, that Jesus was a Jew, and that Jews did not believe, like we Christians did, that Jesus was the Messiah. I set my confusion in the same dark corner where I put the inconceivable and creepy concepts of the Virgin Birth, the Crucifixion, and Holy Communion. The thought of consuming the body and blood of Christ agitated my already nervous stomach into distended indigestion and unchecked farting.

In grade school, I had a Jewish classmate named David, son of a doctor. Of all my classmates, I remember him most fondly, an olive-skinned, quiet boy with nimble moves when we played hide-and-seek chase at recess. During morning prayers and the lunch time blessing, David stepped into the broom closet and pulled the door closed behind him. Why was the class made to do something that sent David into the Goliath of the broom closet? "Ask no questions" was a cultural norm, so my interrogatives just cycled around on the ferris wheel in my mind. Sometimes they were swinging in the wind far off the ground and sometimes they were close enough to touch, but those questions never went away. My inner ferris wheel was loaded with wonders and worries that kept me in a state of anxiousness. What was wrong with my brain?

As I grew older, little was required of me but to help with the household chores, be a good student, and obey grownups. The time was long in coming

---

[15] A derogatory term used to label a person who does not acknowledge the God of Christianity

before I realized that some adult demands didn't square with a key command of Jesus, a biblical rule I was also expected to follow. *Do unto others as you would have them do unto you.*[16] A confusion of messages kept nudging my secret investigation into all that wasn't making sense, including the machinations of my own mind.

White Delta society fostered the Southern lie that claimed separate was equal. Years passed since Jackson and its surrounding communities had desegregated their schools, but the sloth of justice had not yet arrived in Clarksdale. A full six years after Debra Lewis's parents registered her for first grade in Carthage, Clarksdale was finally forced to make plans for integration. From what I overheard at church dinners and prayer meetings, where integration was concerned, the general consensus among White Baptists was "Lord, have mercy." On whom, I wondered.

Although I don't have the numbers, I know from eavesdropping on my mother's conversation with friends that the most talented teachers in our town ended up with private school contracts. I also remember overhearing my father explain to my mother that if I were to stay in public school for seventh grade, I would be in classes with colored[17] boys who could be as old as seventeen. The stigma worn by Black males had already infected even the most level-headed gentlemen, at least that's what I believed Daddy to be. Rumor and fear scooted me into a Baptist private school[18] along with a third of my friends. Others attended the secular Lee Academy or moved away to more resistant municipalities.

I learned that the best I could do to fit in was to be better at listening than talking and to comply with the rules demanded of all children: say yes

---

[16] The Golden Rule is the principle of treating others as you want to be treated. This aspiration toward reciprocity can be found in most religions and cultures.
[17] *Colored* is an ethnic slur historically used in the U.S. to denote non-White persons.
[18] Private school enrollment in the state of Mississippi soared from 23,181 students in 1968 to 63,242 students two years later.

ma'am and no sir, please and thank you. I also learned to accept "because I said so" as a reasonable adult answer to my most frequently asked question, which stretched into two long syllables, "Whyyy-eeee?"

My first attempts at being a private investigator were discreet. The emerging Age of Aquarius barely made a dent in my good girl persona, but I wanted to delve deeper into the swiney, wormy wretchedness of the world. A school-bus yellow bumper sticker on a camper van that I had seen at Dairy Heaven flew like a flag on my mental ferris wheel. *Question Authority*, it read.

First came the bell bottoms, then the transistor radio.[19] How I ever talked my parents into getting me a radio and batteries for Christmas, I'll never know. That transistor gave me a chance to enter a world I wanted to understand. Suddenly, I could pretend to be a flower child and learn Three Dog Night, The Carpenters, and The Temptations songs by heart. I could listen to the news reports of church bombings and protest marches and the body counts from Vietnam. When the weather was right, I could pick up a radio station all the way from Chicago. With my new cordless connection to the times, I could travel outside of the boundaries that had been constructed for me and get some of my questions answered on the sly. Grownups weren't the only ones who could keep secrets. My parents, neighbors, teachers, and classmates would never have to know all that I could learn without them.

The disc jockey at the one-man radio station called us girls from the west side of town the Big Five. We dropped in at the station every weekday morning on our long walk to Clarksdale Baptist School to make a request that would air before our seventh-grade day began. Armed with my transistor, we belted out our requested tunes from Casey Kasem's Top 40 list like rock stars.

The Big Five had been together since second grade. We would have numbered seven, but two friends abandoned us for another private school. We tolerated each other's strengths and weaknesses. For years, we produced variety shows in Candy's backyard using sheets on her clothesline as the

---

[19] The transistor radio was one of the most popular electronic communication devices of the 1960s and 1970s.

curtain. We rotated the repertoire so we could each shine at one time or another and reluctantly let Ellie and Candy's little brother have an act. We set up lawn chairs and invited our mothers (except for the church secretary and the nurse, who worked during the day) and the kids from the big Italian family down the street. When we weren't at church or school or doing shows, we planned beauty pageants, watched *Dark Shadows*, and played Truth or Dare. Without my gal pals, I would have had little to spark my imagination. School was not a beehive of creativity and neither was church. We kept learning the same things over and over again. How many times do I have to learn what a noun is, I wondered? The library served as inspiration when my friends weren't around. Aside from the Big Five and my radio, I learned that library books could also teach me to think about life beyond my house, the classroom, and the sanctuary.

Back when I was twelve, my greatest wishes were to shave my legs and wear lipstick. Momma had taken the cue and fulfilled what I insisted was to be my two-part passage into preteendom. She assured me that once I started shaving my legs I wouldn't be able to stop, and with her electric razor, the chore wouldn't be painless. As far as lipstick, she let me have an Avon pink-tinted lip gloss from the Sweet Honesty line, created with whiny twelve-year olds in mind. In exchange for those gifts, she asked me to join her for an afternoon talk she planned for when Ellie was at Brownies.

Momma guided me into the dining room where she unfolded a map-sized poster that spread across the table. She found it at the library. "This is a diagram of what women look like on the inside." she explained. The picture called to mind a cow skull. She pointed out the uterus and the ovaries, explaining the release of an egg and the dispelling of the bloody lining when the egg went unfertilized. She called it menstruation, but told me that some people just called it a period, which made me cringe, the innocence of a punctuation mark forever destroyed. Her lecture ended with that tidbit. For the rest of the details, she gave me a Christian book about "growing up" that described intercourse in terms absent of lust. I couldn't understand how a man and lady "rubbing" each other caused babies, no matter how many times

I read the sentence. If a stork didn't bring babies and rubbing didn't make any sense, when would I ever learn the truth?

I drew up the courage to interrogate Candy about the lecture my mother had given me. "Oh, that?" Candy said. "It's GROSS!" She had a sister already in high school, so her family went on high alert when Aunt Rosie[20] visited. "Did you know that once you start bleeding, you can have BABIES?" Candy bragged. Before long, the blabbermouth spread the news to my group of friends that I had gotten "the talk." One at a time, each of my buddies confessed to me that they had already "started." When would I?

---

[20] One of many euphemisms for menstruation

eight

The religious architecture that stood across the street from our home was the hub of the wheel around which life rotated. Our family attended like many others in our neighborhood did—whenever the doors were open. I rose through the ranks of every activity and when I was old enough, I qualified for Sword Drill.

Imagine this. Several twelve-year olds of varying sizes and shapes, more girls than boys, stand in a ruler-straight line in a church classroom waiting for direction. The girls wear dresses, mostly homemade calico with lacy collars. The boys wear white button downs and dress slacks, church clothes, as they were called then.

On our first night of practice we met in a familiar room where Mr. Springer, an older, single man, had us shove the front row of chairs aside to reveal a line of weathered masking tape that had been there ever since I could remember. *So this is what that's for,* I thought. With much seriousness, he arranged us behind the tape facing out from the chalkboard in a single line. The large son of our family doctor and the tallest of the girls, who was me, Mr. Springer placed as awkward bookends. He staggered the slighter members like uneven twigs between us.

We qualified for the squad by memorizing the books of the Bible and had also been given a number of verses to learn by heart. Our parents signed off on the two pages of rules and so had we.

"Let's open with a song, children." Mr. Springer pulled out a pitch pipe to my surprise. "I can't think of a better one to kick off the Sword Drill season," he added. With that he took the pose of a choir director and blew a B flat. Mr. Springer started marching in place and encouraged us to do the same, which we reluctantly did. At the lift of his arm, we began to sing,

"Onward Christian soldiers, marching as to war—with the cross of Jesus going on before."

"Good job, soldiers," he said with a self-congratulatory grin. We silently straightened ourselves behind the tape line and waited for the next order.

"Did you read the rules, Miss Sharon?" Mr. Springer asked as he placed a regulation Bible in my hands, one that reminded me of the Gideon Bibles I had seen in the drawers of hotel rooms where my family stayed on our way to visit our grandmas.

"Yes, sir," I offered in instinctual reply.

We stood holding our swords[21] loosely at our sides, waiting for our leader's signal. "Attention!" he bellowed. At that, he explained that we should take one aggressive step forward. We followed his command and adjusted our posture, steadying our weapons at our right sides. I couldn't help but feel the disadvantage of being the only left-handed warrior in the bunch. Then we froze like battle-ready statues. So far, so good, I thought to myself. As a good listener with a nervous stomach, even though I studied the rules for days, I digested his directions with more than an ounce of worry.

Satisfied with our collective response as new recruits, Mr. Springer continued with only momentary delay. "Draw swords!" he shouted. For the next action, he showed us a picture from the official manual. We mimicked the illustration by holding our Bibles between our hands near our belly buttons.

"Remember, thumbs and fingers must not extend over the edge of the Bible cover!" Mr. Springer reminded us. He went on to explain the final two steps, and I readied myself for attack.

The next directive required thinking, the quicker and more accurate the better. The first person to identify the target would win the points. "Proverbs 3:5," the Drill master announced as he pulled a stopwatch out of his polyester pants pocket. We had twenty seconds to hit the target of locating the verse. According to the rules, the prompt would be repeated twice, and sure enough, again we heard the measured tenor tone, "Proverbs 3:5."

I formed a strategy in one second, maybe two. Proverbs followed Psalms, and Psalms was in the smack dab middle of the book with some room for

---

[21] "And take the helmet of salvation, and the sword of the Spirit, which is the word of God." Ephesians 6:17

error. Our instructor started with an easy verse straight from the manual. No need to scare any of us away on the first night of practice. Luckily, this verse was a family mantra. My Grandma Eva wrote it on my birthday cards for as long as I could remember.

Three seconds later, the final word burst from our leader like a battlecry, "Charge!" He clicked on the stopwatch like a good trainer would and the flutter of pages began. The scramble at once revealed who knew the location and who didn't. Those heading for the table of contents were done for. I didn't falter. The race to gain points required a poised step forward with my Sword held open to the correct book and chapter and the right index finger on the correct verse.

I nailed it. First place earned ten points, second place five. I steadily maintained a strong lead.

Along with the Scripture Searching drill, we completed biblical character drills, biblical book drills, unfinished quotation drills, topical drills, and doctrinal drills, which included prompts like, "Find a verse which proves that faith in Christ brings eternal life." That was easy for me: John 3:16, a Sunday school standard.

The simple precision of the activity and its lack of calisthenics made it the perfect game for me. I excelled. I studied the list of verses for hours and created pretend competitions in my bedroom, sometimes enlisting Ellie's help. The spring of my seventh-grade year, I eased my way to the regional and then state competition where I won top honors as the Sword Drill State Winner. What I learned from Sword Drill was that I could accomplish a goal on my own without doing it to please anyone but myself, and that realization excited my soul.

nine

At some point during our first years in Clarksdale, the local newspaper, *The Press Register*, published a personal-interest story about our family that inaccurately made mention of our interest in camping. We had no such interest. Daddy was flummoxed, having said nothing about that sort of pastime, but instead of making a stir, he bought a military-grade tent and started planning summer vacations. He would correct the record by creating documentation to match it. A reporter's goof (or practical joke) facilitated our adventurous travels far from the Land of Cotton.

An epic eastward trip when I was eleven took us to Mammoth Cave, Smoky Mountain National Park, the Outer Banks, Roanoke Island, the Blue Ridge Parkway, Fort Knox, and the homes of Helen Keller, Edgar Allen Poe, and Thomas Jefferson. Daddy's love of nature and history grounded the itinerary and underscored his efforts to inspire and educate his three female passengers. His girls would have plenty to report for the standard "What I Did On My Summer Vacation" assignment when the new school year rolled around.

I remember my fear at living in the canvas contraption held together by metal poles. In North Carolina during a wicked storm, the tent blew over. Thankfully, we hadn't been inside. As much as I wanted my Boy Scout sleeping bag to protect me, my unfettered imagination, fed by Daddy's morality tales of the dangers of hooligans, hitchhikers, and tramps (Dare I say wretches?) suggested otherwise. My bedtime prayers were simple, "Lord, please keep us safe." When morning came, and I smelled the Spam frying on the cook stove, I opened my eyes with confidence that it was my prayer that had done the trick.

Camping itself taught the temporal nature of existence. I never failed to feel a lurch when the tent came down, the tarp came up, and the campsite was absent of any sign of us. *But nobody will know we were ever here*, I brooded.

The summer after my thirteenth birthday, Daddy arranged for our family to camp our way from Mississippi to California, which meant miles of backseat confinement for my sister and me.

For years, Daddy had on alternating Saturdays taken his girls to the segregated Carnegie Library in Clarksdale. A few days prior to our westward journey, he saw to it that we had the chance to restock our reading supplies.

Once we entered the old stone building, I broke away from Daddy and Ellie and skipped my way to the basement staircase. I knew which stairs creaked and where the railing was splintered on the way to the children's section where the smell of books mingled with mildew. I also knew not to clomp too hard lest the handsome librarian think poorly of me. "Mind your manners. You're a Fabriz," Daddy remarked before I entered a public occasion. His reminder reinforced my posture while Momma prompted me to "remember to smile."

What I learned was that Southern charm had nooks and crannies of more menacing things. Not all straight shoulders and grins could be trusted. I fell prey to the shams of others on occasion, but I learned to spot insincerity over time. My mother gave me a word that helped me label the fakes. She called their behavior "two-faced." I swore to myself I would never be like that. Not if I could help it. Momma also taught me when receiving a compliment to always consider the source. Her advice kept me on the lookout for false friends. Books, with their antagonists and betrayals, reinforced her counsel. I learned about the wretches of the world in pages from the fiction section. The imaginations of others also taught me that not every story had a happy ending.

My eyes scanned the shelves that had grown so familiar to me. Over the years, I moved from picture books to chapter books with pictures to books with no pictures at all. As I began a calculated search for the stories that would travel with me, I spotted a well-worn paperback sitting askew on a high table. In those days, paperbacks weren't common in the children's area and neither were unshelved books, so I moved closer to take a look. Why would a diary be printed for other people to read? I wondered. I had my own diary, one locked with a key, but mine was safely hidden from view and would never end up in a library. Curiosity extended my reach, and I added the book to my stack.

I arrived at the circulation desk and greeted the swan-necked librarian. She rewarded me with the glorious half-moon smile that formed ridges of wrinkles in her cheeks like a tide of happy waves. She traded me hundreds of books over the years, and I never tired of the vista of her face.

"I'm taking all these books to California!" I bragged.

She beamed. With a guarded grin, she stamped my latest choices, including the *Diary*, and wished me an adventure. She called out to me when I was at the base of the stairs, "Sharon, you're old enough to check out adult books when you return." I gave her an awkward wave as those words landed hard in my belly. Go upstairs with the grown ups? Why would I want to do that?

The day of departure filled me with joy. I packed my red plaid satchel with pencils, paper, and my library finds. Ellie carried a sackful of Archie comics, coloring books, and crayons. Daddy tossed in our bed pillows. Momma held her sunglasses and Daddy's sack of apples. We were ready to cross state lines all the way to the Pacific. Our station wagon pulled a used pop-up trailer that Daddy bought, practical man that he was. I hoped the trailer's metal casing would protect us from intruders and end my late-night jitters, ones that often kept me awake and anxious, even in the safety of my own bed.

As we crossed the Mississippi River into Arkansas a short half-hour from home, I reached for the paperback that caught my attention a few days before. I examined the cover and flipped through the pages. The whole story was in diary entries? Weird. Would the small type be too hard to comprehend? I told myself to tackle it one sentence at a time.

Soon I time-traveled to 1942 Amsterdam with a girl named Anne. I did the math. Daddy and Momma would have been ten years old when Anne was thirteen. That blew my mind. By the time Daddy steered us across the Texas state line, I moved into what Anne had named the Secret Annex and was entrenched in the private lives of two Jewish families who were hiding in fear for their lives.

With no map to consult, I had no idea where Amsterdam was except in my vague definition of Europe. I knew nothing of the Holocaust, little of World War II. What I had been taught about the Jews was that they were God's chosen people, another cause for confusion. Why, then, was the Frank family in hiding? I wasn't getting the whole story, but I was bent on figuring out whatever I could. Though the diary denied me much of the context of historical detail that I would learn years later, what it did provide was a grand tour of an unfettered soul.

On January 6, 1944, after Peter, the boy whose family was also in the Annex, asked Anne to tell him about herself, she wrote a curious line. "*I found that it was easier to think up questions than to ask them.*" Her admission startled me. I wanted to write in the margins, "Me, too!" How could she so clearly express what I had been feeling? The novelty of a two-thousand-mile drive to California couldn't hold a candle to Anne's diary. Despite truck stops, Dairy Queens, and historical markers, Anne's life overtook mine, and I adopted her as kin.

With Ellie sleeping on the bench seat beside me, I dissolved into Anne's world of social constrictions, family tensions, young love, and philosophical angst. Her entries would have me in the grit of messy family matters one minute then offer a way to cope the next. "*As long as this exists, this sunshine and this cloudless sky, and as long as I can enjoy it, how can I be sad?*" Anne wrote in the winter of 1944. I leaned my head against the seatback, and there it was outside the back window. Anne and I shared the sunshine and the very same cloudless sky!

Over a hundred pages later as our Chevrolet approached the Mojave Desert, 1944 still had me in the Secret Annex with my enthralling confidant. I was within pages of finishing the diary when I reached the entry dated July 15, 1944, written twenty-seven summers before. Anne assured me that "*parents can only give good advice or put [us] on the right paths, but the final forming of a person's character lies in their own hands.*" I slowed down and pondered that idea. I could form my own character?

In the same entry, she confided that *"ideals, dreams, and cherished hopes rise within us, only to meet the horrible truth and be shattered,"* I hear you, Anne! I thought about the confusion that bubbled in my belly since the assassination of Martin Luther King, the war in Vietnam, and the Kent State massacre.[22] Moth holes kept appearing in my curtained reality, leaving spaces to peek through. If I was brave enough to look, what would I see?

Anne was perceptive and feisty—a bold new voice in my sheltered world, a voice not afraid to ask questions aloud and to make original proclamations, whether other people liked them or not. I curled deeper and deeper into the corner between the back seat and back door, letting the well-worn diary shield my face from the scorching sun. My heart squeezed as I read her next declaration. *"In spite of everything, I still believe that people are really good at heart...."* Could that be true? I had been taught that humans were born sinful creatures and needed to be saved from eternal damnation. Was my heart good or evil? I wanted to believe Anne. I knew I could trust her and decided I would.

"Don't forget to look out the window, Sharon." Daddy reminded me as he munched his afternoon apple. Shameless about the zealous crunching involved, he bore down to the core every time.

"I will, Daddy," I said in a polite reply, "but this book's really good." Already I was sneaking in oppositional "buts" when I could.

Daddy interrupted my reading mid-sentence. I continued processing Anne's words, *"....I simply can't build up my hopes on a foundation consisting of confusion, misery, and death."* Hmmmm. I thought. Me either!

Disneyland and the Pacific were still only fairy tales as the unending desert flattened in all directions. The sun speared into the station wagon, the trailer wobbling behind us. In that barren landscape, I read Anne's final entry. The diary ended like a rip of lightning in a sky absent of clouds. What followed was something called an epilogue. *"Anne and her sister Margot died of typhus in 1945 at Bergen-Belsen just weeks before the end of the War."* Wait. What?! I read and reread the impossible words then poured back through

---

[22] Four unarmed students were killed with another nine wounded at Kent State University by the Ohio National Guard on May 4, 1970. Students were protesting the bombing of Cambodia in the ongoing Vietnam War.

the entries, looking for clues, checking for missing pages. My face pressed against the window, eyes squinting back tears as my belly coiled, ready to strike, but at what? At whom? I fell into a sadness that sunk into my throat and ripped into my gut.

Beside me, Ellie colored a pink puppy in a field of blue daisies, oblivious to the cruelty of the world. Momma's teased hairdo smashed against the window. Was she napping? I wanted to tap her on the shoulder, to be reassured.

"What happens to Jews when they die?" I wanted to have the courage to ask her. But I knew better. That question already had an answer. John 3:16 provided the formula: "For God so loved the world that he gave his only begotten son that whosoever believeth in him shall have eternal life." How many times had I earned points in Sword Drill competitions by knowing that verse? Too many to count.

I was old enough to follow the trajectory of Christian logic. Anne was Jewish. She did not fulfill the qualifications for admission to heaven. Jews did not believe that Jesus was the "only begotten son" who offered "eternal life." In Baptist doctrine, two destinations awaited the dead. For the unsaved, like Anne, the final resting place was not heaven but the Lake of Fire. How could I have anything to do with sending her there?

I held the library book to my chest like a holy grail. Was I to believe the Word of God or the Word of Anne? I weighed John 3:16 against July 15, 1944 and felt how they landed in my tummy. I made a decision. I vowed to my dear comrade that I could not and would not believe in any God who created a hell, much less a God who sent people there for not doing what He said. Resolved, I buried the paperback deep in my satchel and finally found the strength to speak. "I'm looking out the window, Daddy. See?"

Glaring past the parched sage to the vacant sky, now hazy with afternoon heat, I wondered when and how this new God of mine would appear.

ten

My desert illumination upon finishing *The Diary of a Young Girl* heightened my attention and crystallized my skills of observation. Our California vacation began in San Diego, our campsites moving from Chula Vista to Orange County and a parking lot style campground that would be our home during the LA stay.

The day we returned from our Disneyland adventure, "It's a Small World" still dancing in my head, Momma said with worry in her voice, "Leo, there's a note on the camper."

"Oh, george," Daddy mumbled in his favorite faux expletive as he bent himself low, a practiced move to prevent his head from bumping the car frame.

Ellie and I stayed in the car, uncertain of what to do. I decided that there must be a criminal on the loose in the campground or that one of our grandmothers had died. I tended toward the tragic now that I had exposed myself to news of riots and body counts and the general agreement that the world was falling apart. No one was in charge now that I had fired the God who made heaven and hell.

Call your office, the note read. Daddy showed it to us so that we could see for ourselves. "Everything's fine, girls. I'll be right back." He strode away to the pay phone near the entrance.

"Let's start supper," Momma suggested. She lumbered toward the picnic table with a subdued grimace, clearly fatigued after the extreme walking the day of amusement required of her. As she bent toward the ice chest, she started to sing, "You can smile / when you can't say a word / you can smile / when you cannot be heard / you can smile / anytime, anywhere / you can smile, smile, smile." It was Momma's motto and a major hint for us to cheer up and make the best of whatever was ahead. Daddy's motto was a flat statement—"It could be worse."

Momma rolled right into "What a Friend We Have in Jesus," and my stomach rumbled. She was expert at sneaking in sermons on the sly. I was not in the mood for her message. Jesus and I were in a fight. Did he have a hand in heaven's admission rules or was His Father the only one responsible? I had to wonder. Maybe Jesus didn't like the idea of hell anymore than I did. The Trinity concept continued to fluster me. And why, by the way, wasn't there a girl in that trio?

All Daddy would tell us that night as he arranged the charcoal in the grill was that transfer orders were waiting.

I squashed my desire to scream, to pout, to throw myself under the trailer and cry. How could this BE? We lived in Clarksdale for five long years. What about my friends? eighth grade? my future? I stuffed the questions under my appetite and grabbed a handful of Fritos. I filled my mouth and crunched hard until every chip was ground to pulp. Was God bullying me into submission?

The next day, we traveled to downtown Los Angeles where Daddy visited the F.B.I. office. Because of a recent security breach,[23] the rural offices that housed only two or three agents required a reorganization of manpower. Daddy did not inform us of the details. We were moving again and that was that.

What we discovered was that the two-man office in Clarksdale was to be closed, and Daddy would be working sixty miles up the road in a consolidated office in Oxford. We were to move within the month to the home of the University of Mississippi "Ole Miss" Rebels and the first integrated schools my sister and I would ever attend. But first, we made our way to the sequoias, and my eyes were drawn upward in a whole new way. Something told me my new god lived in one of those sensational trees.

---

[23] In 1970, a coordinated effort of the Citizens' Commission to investigate the FBI resulted in a break-in at a small Pennsylvania office that contained files outlining illegal counterintelligence actions taken against groups deemed threatening, including *civil rights organizations and their leaders*. The files recovered were released to the press, and an uprising against the F.B.I. followed.

Daddy placed a box the size of a laundry hamper at the foot of my bed. "Whatever you can fit in this can go," he said. In my thirteen years, my parents moved the four of us around more times than I could remember, but this was the first time that it occurred to me that I could pack for myself.

"What about the rest of my stuff?" I asked.

Daddy hooked his hand over my shoulder and said, "You don't need all those old toys anymore. You're a teenager now." Did he remember the night a few months before when he wished me goodnight with an awkward recognition of a once-in-a-lifetime event? "I understand you became a woman today," he had said, neither of us making eye contact. "Uh-huh," I answered, embarrassed that Momma had told him about my first period. It had come too late to give me any bragging rights with my friends, but I was relieved to be normal. As I grew older, I appreciated Daddy's gesture as brave and sweet. We didn't share many moments like that, and I wouldn't forget it.

I couldn't disagree with Daddy about all the childhood belongings. What thirteen-year-old girl needed stuffed animals or Mr. Potato Head or Barbie dolls. This was an opportunity to grow up. I could see that. What was it the librarian said before our epic trip? I was allowed in the grownup section now.

To cope with the ache that came with the news of the move, I soothed myself with graham crackers and milk. I had a couple requisite crying sessions with my friends, all of whom promised to stay in touch. "We can be penpals!" Candy promised. "Oxford's only an hour away." She batted her red-rimmed baby blues at me like a soap opera star. As it happened, an hour turned out to be the perfect distance for the friendships I had held so dear to fade like the print of a newspaper left out in the sun too long.

I carefully untaped the posters from my closet doors, afraid that the sticky residue left on the wood would get me into trouble. My favorite poster displayed a little boy touching his nose to the nose of a kitten. *Be ye kind* was embossed in the meadow beside them. That Bible verse still made sense to me. I rolled up the poster, deciding to bring it along.

The piano that had been in my bedroom, an oddity of placement that was practical at best, would land in the living room in our new house. I lifted the top off the piano bench and pulled out the sheet music for "Que Sera Sera" and my favorite song book, *The Beatles' Hits Made Easy*. My parents could pack the hymnal in their stuff; it didn't need to take up space in my box. Next, I emptied the bookshelf of my autograph book, diary, and red leather Bible. That's when I heard a knock on the door.

I grabbed my Bible in a nervous fit and leaned back on my pillow with my legs stretched out over the rumple of my bed. "Come in," I said in a voice that cracked a little as I threw the Bible open to the middle, just where I knew Psalms would be.

"Packed up?" Daddy said in his matter-of-fact way.

"Almost." I assured him. I knew he saw the box already filling. The evidence proved me right.

"Whatcha reading?" Daddy asked.

"Just some Psalms," I answered, looking toward the top of the page to confirm that's where I had landed. I hadn't. Whoops. Did Daddy notice?

"The movers will be here first thing in the morning. Let's be ready." Daddy knocked twice on the wall in an exclamation point. "Nightie-night."

"I will, Daddy, don't worry," I yelled as he walked down the hall. I knew how to keep my parents at bay. Do what they ask. Period. It had worked as a survival tactic for years. Cautious, clever, strategic, Those were qualities that I had developed, skills that I had learned by paying attention. Mouth shut, ears open, eyes peeled. Just maybe I had learned that from Daddy.

I looked down at the page I had opened to in my pious scurry. I overshot Psalms by an inch and landed in Isaiah, my Sword Drill skills already rusting. My eyes closed and I let my finger drop onto the page. I played this random game regularly, seeking a horoscope that would meet with my parent's approval. Chapter 40, verse 24. I whispered it outloud, "Yea, they shall not be planted; yea, they shall not be sown; yea, their stock shall not take root in the earth: and He shall also blow upon them, and they shall wither, and the whirlwind shall take them away as stubble." Not too promising. And just who was "they," I wondered. Us and them seemed to populate the Good Book, I concluded. And from what I had learned so far, with that line of thinking, somebody on one side or another was always bound to get hurt.

I thought back to May, to the accomplishments of my seventh-grade year. I had received the Citizenship Award at the promotion ceremony and before that had been named the State Winner of Sword Drill out of all the Southern Baptist Churches in the State of Mississippi—at least all the ones that had a team. All of that notoriety was about to dissolve into nothing. Sixty miles up the road, I would be just another brown-haired girl with a little too much meat on her bones and a foggy future ahead.

eleven

The summer broke me in two, leaving me wary of the kingdom of heaven and maddened by how adults had orchestrated my future into a globby mess. On a quiet July morning, my family took leave from the home we had known for eighty months, forever in childtime. The empty rooms we left behind mirrored my heart as I sat on my knees turned toward the rear window of the station wagon, my identity shrinking as Clarksdale vanished into the horizon.

The novelty of Oxford's hills heightened my interest, and I took to bike riding the nearby campus of the University of Mississippi, affectionately called Ole Miss, a historical expression that slaves used to reference the wives of plantation owners. The connotation is an eerie reminder of the racism embedded in namings far and wide.

My legs had to pump hard to pedal up Sorority Row until I figured out a route that let me coast down it instead. The street of pristine mansions opened onto tree-lined boulevards, all of which seemed to lead to an imposing memorial statue of a confederate soldier. The other prominent campus feature was the football stadium. On game days, when the wind was right, we could hear the cheers from the stands and the band playing "Dixie" in our own backyard.

Ole Miss Rebels[24] football was the talk of the town in '71, the year the team went on to win the Peach Bowl. Daddy scored tickets to a home game that fall. I was doused with taboo-busters right and left, forward and back. Smoking was rampant. Drunkenness was celebrated. Cursing was fashionable. I was both embarrassed and fascinated. Why had Daddy brought us to a sinner's paradise? Fans waved Confederate flags from the stands, cheering

---

[24] *Rebel* is a Civil War term indicating loyalty to the Confederate States

their favorite players, all White as can be.[25] Popular props of racism were a bike ride away from my neighborhood and on display for the world to see, and I still hadn't been educated to their meaning.

During eighth and ninth grades, I grew by inches everywhere. I stood a hand taller than Momma. My nervous stomach rumbled like it had when I was a child. Add to that monthly menstrual cramps that laid me out for at least a day. Momma lent me sympathy and a couple of her pain relievers to get me through the worst of it. Magic! Soon I was stealing one Darvon at a time to amass my own stash, a tactic that lasted through high school. My sense of self warped. Nothing about me was predictable: girl-woman one minute, my temper flaring, woman-girl the next, my pillow wet with tears.

My parents decided that enrollment in the Bible Memory Association would straighten me out. I was made to memorize up to sixteen verses a week using a special lesson book my parents ordered. Every Sunday afternoon, Ellie and I recited our verses to a neighbor, our official checker. She marked our mistakes and assigned us points on a scorecard Daddy mailed in to the Association for prizes. I protested the assignment frequently, locking myself in my bedroom, refusing to come out until I was excused from the weekly chore. I was studying biology and Homer, for goodness sake! How could life be so unfair? My retribution came in the form of a silent rebellion. I wrote poems, coding my feelings in metaphors, and kept them in my school binder secured from prying eyes.

Being at odds with Daddy and Momma waxed and waned. They both had plenty to handle without adding me to the mix. I could see that. Daddy's territory hadn't changed, so his time on the road had doubled. Momma had a leg fusion surgery in Memphis and a long recovery ahead. She was on crutches for months, and her hobbling slowed the household down to a crawl. When the healing was complete, she would be fitted for another brace and her handicap would be even more visible. I was reminded that her

---

[25] Ben Williams would be the first Black player to integrate the team, but not until 1972.

neuromuscular disease was progressing and saw what that meant. My heart ached for her, but I didn't know how to tell her that. Instead, I delivered her coffee in bed and tried to stay out of her hair otherwise.

On the surface, I was the good girl I had always been, but I was also a spy wearing the mask of my former self. We were all putting on brave faces, but misery sat right below the surface. I accepted the fact that nothing was as it seemed. Not even me.

Ellie and I hadn't shared a bedroom for many years, and our closed doors, different schools, and separate social sets kept us distanced in all ways. I felt disconnected with all that I had counted on. I was lonely. Depressed, too.

My school experience was initially unaltered from the segregation I had known in Clarksdale. In eighth grade, I encountered Black students during passing periods only, and then teachers were at their doors, scooting us into classrooms from the long hallway. Honors classes served "qualifying" students and were populated with kids who looked like me.

At lunch, I nabbed an empty chair at the table for four that hosted, besides me, the Star Trek nerd who looked a creature from Mars, the platinum blond who at six-feet tall made my height feel normal, and the pimple-faced daughter of the liquor store owner who lived on the outskirts of town. When the army brat with no butt and a mass of freckles showed up at the door of the cafeteria, we stole a chair from another table and dared anyone to snitch on us. Who else would welcome her into their fold? No telling how much my social life suffered because of those associations. Still, I needed my acquaintances, and they needed me. I accepted that true friends were a thing of the past.

By ninth grade, continued segregation in biology and English classes gave way to a mixed crowd in the course that had no honors counterpart, Mississippi History. The dim classroom felt more like a prison than any I had ever entered. Mrs. Washington's desk was centered in front of a window that looked onto a brick wall, so different from the sunny Honors English classroom. A double row of student desks stood opposite each other, the empty square footage in the midle a ready battleground. Black students filled the desks to the teacher's left and seven of us pale kids had our pick of desks on the right. Mrs. Washington, a rotund Black woman with a serious demeanor, could see the door and all the desks with one turn of her head. I learned to complete my lessons with my eyes glued to the textbook. When we studied the Civil War, I thought I'd get the education I had been needing. I was mistaken. The question of slavery was reduced to lessons on state's rights and the benefits of an agricultural economy.

I don't remember the names of any students in that class and was never closer than twelve feet to any of my Black classmates unless we were turning in our work at the same time. If this was what integration looked like, I wasn't impressed.

Thankfully, the youth group at church became a haven of contemporary thought. The university influence might have infected the atmospheres of even the Baptist churches in town. The teen choir learned and performed the Christian musical *Tell It Like It Is*. I scored a small solo in one of the opening songs. My lines went like this: "Cotton candy clouds, so fluffy and white, who put you there in a sky of deep blue? Or do you just happen to float along, pretty and white in a sky so blue, so blue, so blue." The stanza was empty of the doctrines that punctuated the song's ending and was a perfect fit for my spiritual turmoil. I was singing a question! One day as I was practicing my part at home, Momma called from her sick bed, "What in the world is that song about?"

I answered in my good-daughter voice, "It's called Master Designer, Momma." She didn't answer back, but I thought I heard a "humphhh" before I closed my bedroom door and put on a stack of 45 records[26] to play, starting with "If I Had a Hammer" and "Let it Be."

The youth hymnal our choir used pulled at me like the thesaurus had, and I discovered new songs that didn't mention the blood of Jesus or mighty fortresses. The spiral bound cover sported splashy bubble font and swashes of lime green and hot pink, groovy colors. The collection held titles that didn't repel me: "Put Your Hand in the Hand (of the Man who Stilled the Waters)" and "Pass It On." Hip music hit Christian mainstream. My parents were not fans.

As a result of the upbeat message this fresh music held, I adapted a new way of interacting with the precepts of the Baptist faith. I armed myself with the Bible itself, scouring the New Testament for cool words to put in bubble

---

[26] The most common form of a vinyl two-sided single record, derived from its play speed, 45 rpm.

font and curvy scripts. "He that loveth not knoweth not God; for God is love"[27] became my favorite verse. In a radical move, I switched the He for She. No lightning struck. Maybe I would get the hang of a more contemporary Christian lifestyle and not be completely alienated from what my family believed. Now fifteen, I foresaw a time when I wouldn't be strapped forever to "The Old Rugged Cross."[28]

Near the close of my ninth grade year in 1973, Daddy received new moving orders. We were headed for Dallas. Big city! The news brightened my mood. Malls! Two weeks before our departure that changed. An agent assigned to a considerably smaller East Texas oil town was killed in an auto accident. Daddy would replace the deceased agent, my dream of metropolitan living dashed in what Bob Dylan coined as "a simple twist of fate."

I received the flat reassurance from both my parents that "God's will is God's will." Their united front dismissed my need for sympathy. I would have to seek consolation elsewhere. So would my sister.

---

[27] 1 John 4:8
[28] a popular Christian hymn written by George Bennard in 1912

twelve

Our first month in Tyler, Texas, was spent at the Holiday Inn on the opposite end of town from where we would eventually live. Daddy had purchased a house still under construction, and we would have to commute to and from the hotel for weeks. My first day at Robert E. Lee High School,[29] Daddy dropped me off early, and I paced the school twice to make sure I understood where I was. Red and white cheerleader language lathered the windows. *Red Raiders RULE!*[30] and *'73-'74 to the MAX!*

After a hike across the outdoor campus to the English wing, I arrived at Speech class, a sophomore elective. A mix of Black and White faces already occupied a few of the desks. Okay, I thought. This is different. I slipped into a more conspicuous seat than I wanted on the front row.

Mr. Truluck wore a sports coat, and his wrinkle-free pants skimmed the top of his dress shoes just like a game show host. He addressed students as "Miss" or "Sir" and called out names as if everyone had just won a spot on *The Price is Right*. "Say 'Here!' loud and clear," his radio voice boomed, equal parts carnie and favorite uncle. "Welcome Miss Fabriz, everyone. She's joining us all the way froommmmmm..." and then he paused and pointed a dramatic finger at me.

Embarrassed, I answered on cue, "Mississippi." A grumble escaped from a corner, and I thought I heard the word "honkey."

"Now, now," Mr. Truluck chided and then returned to roll call.

---

[29] A 2016 study from the Southern Poverty Law Center found that 52 schools are named after Gen. Robert E. Lee. "[A]t least 39 of those schools were built or dedicated from 1950 to 1970," the study reports.

[30] The school board had voted the previous year after a Federal Court Order to replace the Rebel mascot, Confederate flag, and the "Dixie" fight song. The school name did not change until 2020.

Would I forever be trapped by my Mississippi roots, double-bound by my accent, so different from the East Texas twang? I kept my mouth shut and the details of my existence to myself. But how long could I do that in Speech class? Who would want to pal around with a Mississippi hick whose father was the law?

During the first weeks of school, I arrived as early as I could to each class, curled into my desk, and opened to the dog-eared page of the longest story I had ever attempted, *Gone with the Wind*. My grandmother bought me the paperback after she treated me to the special movie night when I was in fifth grade. I hadn't yet dared to read it, worried that it would swallow me in its sea of words. The paperback weighed in at over a pound and numbered well over a thousand pages. Now it was an emblem of my insecurity and might be hefty enough to shield me from socializing for the entire semester. I wasn't up for chitchat and couldn't bear the thought of ending up at the losers lunch table ever again.

Hoping to disappear, I instantly sank into the story, oscillating between irritation with chaste Melanie and fickle Scarlett, that is when I wasn't in love with both the saint and the sinner. I was having girl crushes and didn't know it.

Before Speech class one October day, when my dog-ear was within pages of the end and at that awkward place where a massive book gets hard to hold, a hand the color of milk chocolate pushed the paperback down onto my splintered desk. An alto voice laughed, then spoke. Jade. I had been watching her antics, her free-flowing humor, her politically savvy buttering up of Mr. Truluck. "Nice shoes, Mr. TV star!" she'd tease him and then flash a smile that put us all at ease. She had one deep dimple that animated her cheek when she spoke, and she knew how to use it to her advantage. On top of that, her short afro and boy pants intrigued me.

"Now, why would anybody read anything that thick?" she joked.

I uncurled myself and met brown eyes as twinkly as sparklers on the Fourth of July. Every part of her face was a celebration.

I must have been staring because she leaned farther across the aisle and tapped my free hand. "Hey, you," she insisted. "Tell me. Why?"

I couldn't resist her dimple and the way her irises centered themselves on me. "It's kinda hard to explain." I whispered, relieved to see Mr. Truluck still outside the door waving in the tardies.

Her eyes held mine and her fingers lingered on the edge of my desk. "Try me."

We left class together and compared our schedules, agreeing to meet on a bench outside the library during lunch. As we nibbled our sandwiches, I explained the story of how when I was eleven my grandmother had taken me to see the anniversary run of the movie on which the book was based. The more I talked about the story, the more uncomfortable I grew. The realities of plantation life had been lost on me until I heard myself glorifying the protagonists, slave owners all. Jade just shook her head and chuckled. Cutting me short, she interrupted, "Tell me about you." About me? I wondered what to say.

Jade and I became fast friends. We both needed to talk, and we were both ready to listen. That made for a good match. We told our entire life stories to each other, and Jade took it from there. She taught me about the Black radio station in town and showed me a few dance moves. I'd talk to her about church, and she'd put her hand over her mouth to hide a dramatic yawn. She started calling me Shaggy because of my haircut. We wrote to each other and traded letters at lunch. I sprinted to Geometry because that was the class where I read her sweet and clever notes.

I witnessed Momma's kindness to Jade on the one hand and her fear on the other. The fact that Jade was Black complicated matters. I suspect Momma didn't want to appear prejudiced, but she was also guarded. She'd serve up hot meals from a local deli for us when we walked home for lunch, but she'd insist on driving us back to school to reduce the chances of the neighbors seeing us together.

When I spent time at Jade's house, Jade's mom taught me how to cook cabbage Southern-style and took us out to the stables where she kept a horse. She had examined me down to my dress size and seemed pleased that Jade had a White friend not afraid to come all the way up to the Black side of town. Momma drove me, but not without reservations. "You be careful," she'd say. "I'll be back in two hours."

After a couple months of socializing, when Jade told me to meet her in the girl's bathroom ten minutes into the last period of the day, I was confused but willing. Our first kiss was an injection of libido that shook me from head to toe. I had kissed three boys in my lifetime, my first in seventh grade and two others in the boredom of summertime in Oxford, where bike rides on dirt roads near our house led to such things. The difference between their lips and hers was like the difference between cotton and velvet. I had no idea what it meant, but I was more than willing to explore. Jade was no stranger to the female anatomy, unlike me, who didn't even know how to pronounce the word "vagina" until my freshman year of college. And "penis" either, for that matter.

One winter afternoon when Momma picked me up from school, she said she had a question to ask me. The forewarning should have put me on notice. "Is Jade a (long pause) homosexual?"[31]

"No!" I said with a tone of disgust that I delivered like Miss Jane from the *Beverly Hillbillies*.[32] I had no idea what the word meant, but it sounded dirty. The kisses that Jade and I shared in the girls' bathroom during afternoon classes begged to differ, but I was naive to the label. What was the big deal?

Not long after, Momma and Daddy sat me down and told me that our next-door neighbor, who happened to be the high school Assistant Principal, had concerns about my friendship with Jade. We had been seen together when we should have been in class. During P.E., one of the coaches had shooed us out of the girl's showers.

"Were you clothed?" Momma asked.

"Of course, Mother," I answered in veiled disrespect.

I wanted to say that we were just smoking a joint, but that wouldn't have gone over well either.

"These concerns are affecting your reputation, Sharon Hope." Daddy chimed in, folding his hands on the table in a prayerful pose.

What reputation? I wanted to scream. *I haven't had a reputation to affect since we moved away from Clarksdale! Nobody knows who I am or cares. Nobody knows anything about me. You think it's enough for me to go to school and make*

---

[31] In 1973 the board of the American Psychiatric Association voted to remove homosexuality from its list of mental illnesses.
[32] The Beverly Hillbillies is an American sitcom television series broadcast on CBS from 1962 to 1971 on which Miss Jane played a "spinster."

good grades and go to a stinking church where there's no one my age? How am I supposed to even HAVE a reputation? You don't know what I've gone through, and now you want to steal my last friend in the world. Why do you keep taking things away from me?

I didn't say any of it. Not a word. How I felt didn't matter. It wasn't just about me, it was about the family name. The relationship would end. Over and out.

I called Jade that night and delivered the news. After she made her signature "mm-mm-mm" grumble, she only had one thing to say. "White folks." Delivered with disdain. "Goodbye, Shaggy." Then, she hung up.

For weeks, I sulked in my room writing bad poetry and listening to Diana Ross—*Do you know where you're going to? Do you like the things that life is showing you? Where are you going to? Do you know?*[33]

I could only see Jade from a distance now that the new semester had started. I was taking sociology and she was taking art. I started escaping to the library at lunch and kept my doldrums to myself. One day, my pain threshold maxed out, and I walked off campus at lunch and into the adjoining woods. I wore a homemade calico dress, sewn by a lady from church, and my coveted platform heels—soooo *Soul Train*. I didn't care that they made me over six-feet tall. The uneven ground in the woods made walking difficult. I felt like the daughter of Frankenstein. I could do nothing but lie down on the crackling leaves and sob about everything I had lost.

After a time, wrung out and confused, I found my way out to the main road, a busy loop, and walked home, big trucks blowing their horns at me as I clomped along. When I came through the front door with no books, no watch, no expression, Momma gave me a strange look. I understood why when I stole a glance at the clock on the mantle. It read 1:32.

"I'm not feeling well, Momma," I admitted. "I'm going to bed." I dug out a couple Darvons from my stash, cupped some water in my hands from the bathroom sink and gulped the capsules down with a sigh. I hated my faithless, hopeless, Jadeless life.

---

[33] "Do You Know Where You're Going To" is a song written by Michael Masser and Gerry Goffin and sung by Diana Ross, a member of Motown's royalty.

thirteen

Our family's church membership migrated to a small Texas congregation despite the fact that Tyler was the biggest city we had lived in since Jackson. A massive Baptist church sprawled only minutes from our house, but Momma and Daddy steered toward the modest Bible church farther away because it adhered to stricter doctrinal teachings than would the Baptist church with its gym and coffee house. Church would no longer serve as our primary social occasion.

Ellie and I populated the teen department with a couple older kids from another family. We were used as babysitters and Sunday school teachers for the toddlers, and I, with limited skills, was assigned to play the piano for the Sunday night service when the regular pianist was absent. In one fell swoop, the very parents who set us up to rely on the church for our ration of friends, a network of adults who could be trusted, and opportunities for community service eradicated the possibility of all the above just when we needed those advantages the most. Every single payoff of church-going was blasted into heavens never to be seen again.

A few years back, Momma had become obsessed with a pastor who took an overtly patriarchal, militaristic approach. His doctrine was delivered via the U. S. mail all the way from Houston, where his church was based. Boxes of reel-to-reel tapes landed at our front door during the Clarksdale years. A monstrous tape player sat in a dining room cabinet. Over time, reel-to-reels evolved into cassettes. The player shrunk in size, but the booming voice coming from the speakers was as fierce as ever. The Colonel, as he was known to his followers, demanded respect even in audio recordings.

Momma recruited Daddy to listen to the pastor, too. The biblical authority held law enforcement in high esteem. Had that hooked Daddy?

Whatever turned him on, home Bible study became a part of their regular routine. In our household, "to listen" meant to sit "under the Colonel's teachings" for hour-long sessions several times each week. Nothing was allowed to interrupt their time "studying the Word." When the tapes were on play, I huddled in my room, relieved that my parents were otherwise engaged. The lessons contained and consumed them. My imagination was free to roam during the hours and hours Momma and Daddy spent "under the teachings." With the advent of cassettes, the Colonel joined us on roadtrips, too. Anne would not have approved.

Momma recruited friends in every city we lived to join her in Bible study. She was a missionary and inhabited that role by enlisting friends to hear the "truth of the Word." In Clarksdale, she recruited Ida. In Oxford, Meredith. In Tyler, she found Beth, the woman who lived up the hill in an elegant custom home with her lawyer husband and two perfect children, a girl and a boy. Momma was a living example of the power of The Word. Her neuromuscular disease and her elevated social position as an F.B.I. wife made her a reliable source for the deliverance of truth.

Momma's home life wasn't rich with affection, but she bubbled over with passion. What's a woman to do when her love isn't reciprocated by her mate? She shares it with others, if she knows what's good for her. And that's what Momma did. She shared her bright-eyed wonder at the mercies of the Lord. She rose with the Father's promises on her lips every morning. How else would she be able to get out of bed? She fetched friends, found the intimacy she needed, and held those friendships together with the Power of the Lord. I felt jealous of Momma's friends, who got the best of her. She delighted in their company, laughed with them, and celebrated that "where two or three are gathered together in [Jesus'] name, there [is He] in the midst of them."[34]

The Colonel provided a whiff of togetherness between Momma and Daddy, too. That must have been part of Momma's plan. Both parents filled notebook after notebook with doctrinal exclamations while bookcase shelves filled with tapes and publications from the Colonel. On every book back, a thumbprint photo displayed the author in full military dress. The dogma of the pastor's stance filtered into all aspects of our lives. The husband was the

---

[34] Matthew 18:20

head of the household, the wife was second in command, and children were to be seen and not heard.

By the time we lived in Tyler, Momma and Daddy had been entrenched in the Colonel's teachings for several years. They were fired up by the biblical guru and followers at the cost of the social and emotional needs of their daughters. Ellie and I were left to manage ourselves without the one thing we needed: a place to belong.

During my sixteenth summer in 1974, no grand vacation awaited me. Had Daddy been freed from the obligation to show off his camping hobby now that we had moved out of Mississippi or was he smart enough to know that a roadtrip with sixteen and fourteen year old daughters was a recipe for trouble?

The wife of a church elder, who was also a fan of the doctrinal teachings of the Colonel, volunteered to sponsor a small study group for three teenage girls, including me. My parents forced the issue. I joined the meetings to hear the Colonel's entire series of cassette tape lessons extolling the doctrine of Right Man, Right Woman. The scaffolded teaching rose to a climax that promised me a husband at the end of a straight, narrow way that looked nothing like the Yellow Brick Road. All that was required of me was a compliant spirit and guaranteed protection against needing to think for myself.

I digested the content with paper, pen, and a Bible by my side and acted my part like a pro, parroting the primary colors of doctrinal truth with the best of them. Compliance would be my cover and Saturday nights would be my reward. My questions rocketed skyward, tearing holes in the Colonel's high-minded logic. Was there really only one person, one man, in the entire world meant for me? One slip up and I'd lose my chance to meet him? What if he screwed up first? Would I be damned to life as a spinster? My questions exceeded the limits of my patience. Right Man, Right Woman? Whether I knew it or not, I was on a mission to disprove the dogma.

fourteen

Wandering our tranquil neighborhood wasn't unusual for me. I often roamed my way to the bottom of the hill until I met the open path to the loop where traffic hustled by. One Saturday afternoon a silver Cutlass waited at a pull-out three blocks away.

Inside was Reggie, loose afro and all. Our connection was Jade. She and Reggie went way back. Cousins, however distant. He had seen us around school together before the gavel came down on our friendship. A lucrative business, kinship. He wanted an introduction.

When Jade approached me between classes one day, I reprimanded her. "No, Jade! Leave me alone." I pushed her shoulder in full view of whoever might be watching. I didn't need the assistant principal making another visit to my parents.

She held her hands together in prayer with a slip of paper between them. "Please? Please? Pretty please?" she sounded desperate. Her dimple quivered as she bit her lip. What was at stake for her I would never know.

Disappointing Jade seemed impossible, so I took Reggie's number and called him that night. If Daddy knew, he would kill me. A date with a Black guy? No way!

My white skirt slid onto the red vinyl seat while Reggie turned up the volume on the radio as Marvin Gaye crooned, *Let's get it on*. Reggie flashed a devilish smile of perfect teeth in my direction, "Girl, you FINE!"

I remembered that Momma had taught me when flattered to consider the source. Since I knew nothing about Reggie but that he was related to Jade, I let the words go straight to my head. "No I'm not," I smiled, my tone contradicting my words.

The Cutlass took the highway out past town to a street I'd never seen and then onto the dusty gravel lot of a ramshackle motel. Wait. What? My words got caught in my throat. What was happening?

Reggie climbed out first and motioned. A key dangled from his hand. I stepped onto the gravel and looked around for signs of life. "Ummmm." was all I could say. One other car was parked near the office. The only place I had seen rundown hotels like this was in movies, scary ones.

Opening the door, Reggie showed me in. The room pulsed crimson, the twilight urging itself through translucent red curtains. I searched the scarlet shadows for a chair, but the low bed rested alone. The bathroom door slammed shut. All of a sudden I thought about the fact that I had no money, no identification, and no knowledge of where I even was. From the bathroom came the sound of a zipper, the clank of metal, and a running water. When the door creaked open, I saw a naked man in a full profile I had never imagined.

That's when the light switch clicked. Something bad was happening, and I had no escape. What little sense of self I had disembarked my body and perched to watch from a corner of the room.

"Hey, baby. Let's have some fun." Reggie announced. He pulled me up toward the pillow and we kissed. His hair smelled like Jade's, and I breathed in the scent like medicine. In short order, I was under him, his hands jerking my panties past my thighs. "Oh, yeah." he repeated as I became a receptacle, a ride. Pain held me rigid. "Relax, baby," he said. "Just relax." My head was turned toward the window, mouth open, eyes salty. I thought of Jade and why I had made the call. In rhythm to the scene on the bed I silently chanted, *I'm doing this for her I'm doing this for her I'm doing this for her.*

On the return trip, the Cutlass bumped over cracks in the asphalt to the slow, hard guitar licks of B.B. King. *The thrill is gone.* Nothing had prepared me for that day. All I knew was that I was a shameful....wretch!

Dusk settled as I snaked my way back home. I slipped through the den to the bellows of Lawrence Welk's accordion.[35] Daddy rested in his recliner, eating an apple. He raised his hand in a limp welcome, but he didn't speak. To whatever fed his disinterest, I was weakly obliged.

---

[35]Lawrence Welk was an American musician, accordionist, bandleader, and television impresario, who hosted the television program "The Lawrence Welk Show" from 1951 to 1982.

I washed and rinsed my hair three times that night and dressed in the softed flannel pajamas I owned. Then, I slipped my red leather Bible under my pillow and cried myself to sleep.

From that day on, I flew into the ignorant fornications of youth defined first and foremost as sex between a girl and a boy, giving little thought to consequences like pregnancy. I hid my disdain for myself in obscure, dramatic poetry, keeping up flatline appearances around the dinner table and at church. I had adopted a risky, two-faced lifestyle in a time when mental health resources for teenagers were slim and talk of the realities of depression were nonexistent.

Jade was a dream from the past, and Reggie had moved on to fresh bait. My inner life shredded into pieces and confusion became my status quo. I experienced racing thoughts, layers of them, and taught myself to lay on my bed, cover my head with my pillow, and count to ten slowly to calm down. I snuck out of the house on Saturday nights to join a *mixed crowd* from the other high school in town whom I had met through acquaintances of acquaintances once removed. They furthered my foray into mindlessness. I shudder to think of the many times I ran up the street to our house in the middle of night keeping my fingers crossed that the laundry room door on the side of the house was unlocked like I had left it until, by the grace of all that is sacred, I made it safely back inside.

fifteen

I knew I had gone too far when I woke one Sunday morning to Daddy kneeling on the floor beside me, cleaning up my vomit. I noticed I was still in my clothes from the night before. Embarrassment kept me quiet.

A squirt bottle in one hand and a funky towel in the other, Daddy said only one thing to me as he left the room, "Time to get ready for church, Sharon Hope Fabriz." The use of my full name signaled his disgust. He was reminding me who I was.

When I peeked into Ellie's room, her bed was empty and made, two uncharacteristic weekend occurrences. "Where's Ellie?" I yelled down the stairs. When nobody answered, I threw on my robe and found Momma in the kitchen holding a mug of coffee with both hands and staring trancelike out the window onto the treeless backyard.

"She left a note on her pillow. We think she's with Laurie, but we don't know for sure." Momma put the mug in the sink without rinsing it.

"Mom!" I felt like I was always the last one to know what was going on. "Why didn't you tell me?"

"You were asleep until just now." Daddy clearly hadn't told her about the mess beside my bed. "We leave in twenty minutes. Go get dressed." Her monotone rivaled Daddy's. We had turned into a family of zombies and one of us had gone missing.

"So, we're going to church anyway? That's ree-dic-u-lous!" I snapped at her even though I saw the fatigue in her eyes. "We need to find Ellie!"

"Your father has made the decision. Go get ready now." Her voice had taken on as much authority as she could muster.

"I can't believe this is happening!" I yelled as I mounted the stairs. Where was my sister and why did she leave? Was I the reason? She had pulled away from me when Jade came on the scene. Or had I pulled away from her? Our recent interactions had ranged from the silent treatment to flat out physical violence. We had pushed each other around, pulled each other's hair, and I had made her cry more than once with my badgering about her messy habits. Once she had come home from a school trip and found that I had cleaned out her closet, swept the old fast food wrappers out from under her bed, and thrown away the piles of *Teen* magazines she had collected over the years, all the way back to David Cassidy. She was livid.

Why had I been so mean, so disrespectful of her private space? Had I been incapable of pulling myself together enough to feel empathy for my own flesh and blood? Over the years, I had done my best to dim the spotlight put on me because of my academic accomplishments and musical involvements, but I had also been selfish, rarely including her in my own fun and games with friends. I had been a terrible older sister. Ellie didn't owe me an explanation when she ran away. She didn't owe me anything and I knew why.

We had been forced to endure a multitude of transitions that left us to figure out life for ourselves. If she was anything like me, she was feeling the hurt of being torn from the familiar, from home, time and time again.

Ellie returned in a day or two in an uneventful reunion. Familiar routines returned. Our family performed in predictable patterns, but the flagstones had shifted beneath our feet.

There were other disruptions over the years. Shall I begin at the start? I stole when I was ten. At least that was what Daddy made me think I did. I was at Woolworth's, a dime candy bar on the checkout counter, just getting my change back from the quarter that was my allowance. I felt a tap-tap-tap on my shoulder. Daddy. He gave me a smirk and shook his head like I better remember never to get caught buying something as frivolous as candy with my allowance again. From then on, I took to keeping secrets. Maybe something like that had happened to him, too. Were Daddy and I both bound by a vow to go under the radar so we didn't risk the shame of a tap-tap-tap on the shoulder?

In '75-'76, during my senior year, I met an amazing guy at a weekend Distributive Education[36] regional conference. I had slimmed down and taken to walking like a model, tall and proud. My high cheekbones, upturned nose, and hazel eyes suddenly became marketable assets. Lamar was the president of his senior class, as handsome as Sidney Poitier[37] and was both witty and kind. I danced with Lamar during the evening disco party, our bi-racial pairing exciting the crowd. I ended up sneaking into his hotel room, listening to guitarist Jeff Beck on the turntable he had brought along, and feeling the dignity of choice about who I was, who I was with, and why.

Lamar and I kept up the relationship long distance. We lived three hours apart, so phone calls were our lifeline. We talked at all hours, mostly with me calling him. I was the one with a private line, a debatable decision on Daddy's part. Ellie and I shared the phone that was intended to sit on the carpet in the upstairs hallway between our rooms. I took full advantage of the long cord and kept the phone in my room unless Ellie demanded it.

One night, while I was slogging through T. S. Eliot's "The Hollow Men" for English class, I heard Daddy's feet thunder up the stairs. He fanned a piece of paper in my face with the force of a tornado, then let it drop beside me. The phone bill. A list of calls to Denton had been circled with a total written beside them. $100.[38] "Who have you been talking to?" Daddy shouted.

"Uhhhh......a guy?" I answered with trepidation. At least he could be glad it wasn't a girl.

"You'll pay every penny, young lady. Starting now. Give me ten dollars." He held out his large, waiting palm. I went to my top dresser drawer, careful not to uncover my birth control pills, pulled out my wallet, and counted out ten singles. "Nine more payments. Due weekly, by george!" he demanded.

With equal resolve, when he left my room, he bent low and ripped the telephone cord out of the wall, throwing the entire contraption down the stairs. It dinged and bumped to the bottom, receiver tumbling behind. I had never seen him so angry. I realized that I had pushed him over a limit that I doubt he even realized he had.

---

[36] a special high school program of vocational education in which a student is employed part-time, receiving on-the-job training
[37] Hollywood icon Sidney Poitier was the first African-American to win an Academy Award for Best Actor, receiving the honor in 1964.
[38] In 2020 dollars, that translates to $481.60.

My guess is that Daddy investigated the phone number, had a local agent do a drive-by, and learned what he could about "the guy." With all Lamar had going for him, Daddy should have been impressed.

Daddy collected my bill every Saturday and cancelled my last payment for good behavior. At least there was that. In a lighter moment, once my debt was paid, Daddy took me aside and asked to see a picture of "the guy." I lied and said I didn't have one, when in truth I had a copy of Lamar's senior portrait in my wallet. Daddy was testing me, and I didn't care. I figured he knew all about Lamar, and I wasn't about to get sucked in to his investigation.

sixteen

I earned my own money since fifth grade when I started babysitting for fifty cents an hour. I established a thriving weekend business by word-of-mouth in Clarksdale and Oxford. Luckily, word of mouth spread, and I became a popular resource among the young professor set at Ole Miss.

My abilities of observation were sharpened by being in other people's homes. Their bookshelves and magazines looked a whole lot different than ours. Two notable educational tools I scoured with interest were copies of Playboy magazines and the ubiquitous yellow paperback of the times, *Everything You Ever Wanted To Know About Sex* (* But Were Afraid To Ask)*.[39] Once my charges were asleep in their beds, I stretched out in a recliner and took to research like a fish to water.

Since early in my senior year, I worked at J.C.Penney through the same Distributive Education program that had introduced me to Lamar. I was thankful to leave campus after three morning classes for an afternoon in the Gift Wrap, Credit, and Layaway department. At work, I learned from a whole new set of voices, women who had been in the department for decades and male employees who harassed me regularly for being so naive and sweet.

The first sexual assault of the three I would experience in as many years happened with a guy from the automotive department. He called our office often for credit approvals. Whenever I took the call, he gave me a hard time about my accent being so sexy. One day he asked me to have lunch with him. We had never met in person, so he told me where his car was and to meet him there. After I put on my seatbelt, I noticed the sweat on his upper lip as he groped for my hand. He was chubby and short, that I could tell. "It's great to see you." he said. Why was I getting into a car with a guy yet again and giving

---

[39] No. 1 best-seller in 51 countries with more than 100 million readers worldwide; by David Rueben, M.D., 1969.

up my control? We ended up at a small suburban house where he drove into the garage and then guided me straight into a nearby bedroom. A portrait of his family hung from the wall near the bed. A wife. Children. How old was this man? How stupid was I?

"Are we having lunch?" I asked him.

"Lunch?" He looked at me like I was crazy, unbuckled his belt and smiled. "Yeah, we're gonna have lunch," he laughed.

Why didn't I speak up? Say no? Fight him off? Young, naive, ignorant. You name it. I was skill-less and had no tools in my self-protection toolbox.

As a result of a series of abuses, I lived with self-hate and guilt until one day in the far future, I saw myself more as a survivor and less as a good girl gone very, very wrong.

Even though I received a personal letter of invitation from the head of the English Department at University of Houston, Daddy would have none of it. He refused my wishes after we toured the campus when he saw what side of town the school was on. "This is not the place for you, Sharon Hope. Let's keep looking."

A small Christian college five hours from Tyler in northwest Arkansas was more amenable to him, so I reluctantly agreed. Daddy paid my tuition with savings bonds that he counted out in front of me at the beginning of the semester. Until that first round of tuition was due, he hadn't told me that he had started a college savings plan for me when I was a child. Why did he keep such a motivating fact to himself for so long? He hadn't even approached the idea of college with me until well into high school. His silence on the matter reinforced the idea that a woman's place was in the home. College was strictly a place for women to earn their MRS. titles.

I ended up leaving Arkansas midway through my sophomore year and moved back home. My parents didn't know it, but I was in crisis mode once again. Another sexual assault, too many parties, and a lack of boundaries had me hearing voices in my head, unfriendly ones. Daddy and Momma never asked me details, but my transcript spoke for itself. I started my last fall semester with eighteen credits and ended it with six. Daddy's savings bonds had been wasted, and his silence translated to disgust.

Since I was available, I was put on a bus to Minneapolis to assist Grandma Sig as she recovered from a broken ankle in the ice and snow of winter. The weeks with her dried me out and made me take a hard look at myself. I had put on thirty pounds and felt like a blob. I was a mess, and I knew it.

"Not all of life is easy," Grandma said to me one day. She never once invoked pity by talking about her own tragic girlhood or the fact that she had been a widow for a full twenty years. She let me steep in her words and gave me space, saddened as she must have been by my ballooning weight and my pallid complexion.

One day after grocery shopping, I drove myself to Minnehaha Falls. I hugged my ill-fitting coat in the bitter wind and stared at the unmoving ice that hung in great sheets from the top of the creek to the pool below. I hadn't seen The Falls frozen for years, not since the Christmas trips we made to Grandma's when I was a child. Memories of happier times, summer picnics in this special place, warmed a little spot deep in my heart. I needed to pull myself together. I hated the two-faced person I had become. No one in the world knew me for who I was, a lost and lonely soul.

After two months of Grandma therapy, I returned to Tyler and planned to start school again in the summer at a local branch of the University of Texas. I was hired to work at the university library, a most amazing development that boosted my confidence and my motivation to use the brains I had been given. As I was shelving books one day, I came across a guy in the Humanities stacks. I noticed his budding beard, his golden hair, his long, muscular legs. I could see the title of the book in his hand, *Man's Search for Meaning* by Victor Frankl. He noticed me, too. "Nice shoes," he said of my platform sandals. With a curious lift to my voice, I said thanks, and that was our start. We were intellectual equals and both frustrated with the backasswardness of East Texas. Our commiserations were addicting.

One Sunday, I invited Ray to come to church with me. He needed to know what he was getting into. When we arrived home from the service, he asked if he could lie down for a while.

"Y'all go ahead and eat dinner without me," he apologized. Daddy showed him to the guest room where Ray stayed for over an hour. When I asked him about it, he just shook his head and said, "The sermon nauseated me." Bingo. If that didn't deserve a big hug, nothing did.

Weeks later, when Ray asked for my hand in marriage, Daddy said, "No. She's not ready."

Now twenty-one, I fought back. "I'm an adult, Daddy. Ray and I are getting married whether you like it or not." Right Man, Right Woman be damned. I needed a way out of my hopelessness. I married Ray in the chapel of the Baptist church up the street within ten months after our first date.

seventeen

Ellie and I both took the defiant route down the aisle. We hadn't achieved the Right Man/Right Woman payoff that the doctrinal investments of our parents had promised. Ellie and a fellow she had met during her freshman year of college exchanged vows within a year of my marriage to Ray.

Once we girls were on our own, Daddy requested a transfer back to the Twin Cities to be near his mother, Grandma Sig, who was nearing eighty. Momma was nonplussed about the move. She had settled into a life of her own over the nearly ten years of living in Tyler, but move they did, to a two-story house that required her to travel a flight of stairs at least twice a day to get from and to the master bedroom. With her disease progressing and weakness ensuing, her new home in Minnesota was less of a haven and more of a mean joke. Not to mention that her unsteady feet would be challenged by winters of ice and snow.

Momma and Daddy weren't around for the happy occasions of welcoming their firstborn grandchildren into the world, and it seemed that as mothers Ellie and I would be as isolated as our parents' had been when they moved South for Daddy's job.

I flew to Minneapolis with nine-month old Brad for a dutiful trip to the grandparents. Momma had arranged for me to have an afternoon out. I was scheduled for a perm to bolster my '80s must-have hairdo. I left Brad with Momma and drove myself to an afternoon of indulgent primping.

After months of full-time mothering, I was ready to enter a salon space, a predictable haven with the promise that I would look better going out than

I did coming in. My spatial sense helped me arrive without incident. I scored street parking in front of the salon called Blondie's.

"Sharon?" A short, muscular woman with cropped hair extended her hand. "I'm Sal." I was mildly disappointed that I had no time to thumb through the pile of magazines on the coffee table, but instead I smiled and followed Sal to the shampoo sink. "So you're Mary's daughter. She's such a doll." Sal's upper arms flexed with every scrub. "You're lucky to have her."

"Yes, I am." I pictured Momma's obstetrician patting her swollen belly and saying *This baby is lucky to have such a peach for a mother.* I had been reminded of her sweetness over the entire course of my life. I couldn't argue with what was true.

Sal switched to cold water for the final rinse. "Thank God your dad is moving out soon. What do you think about their separation?"

I squeezed my eyes shut as the water chilled my scalp. *What did she say? Did I hear what I think I heard?* I replayed her words.

"Whatever makes them happy," I said in a gust of surprise, my eyes still closed. I wasn't about to open them yet.

"Leo can't give her what she needs. It's his generation." She massaged a towel over my skull, patting it in sync with her pronouncements. "He can't get in touch with his feelings. And he wasn't even in the war."

Her words wound around inside me as she twisted my hair onto the faded blue curling rods. I pictured Daddy carrying Brad in his Snuggly at the zoo the day before. Had I missed the clues? I spent the next two hours calculating and recalculating what I did and didn't know. What about Daddy's losses? Had he made what he wanted out of his life? What did the marriage mean to him?

The perm turned out frizzy, but I gave a fat tip to Sal. Like it or not, she was a source of information I needed. I wonder if Momma ever confronted her about dropping the juicy bomb on my unsuspecting head.

When I returned home, Momma greeted me with her usual smile. "Oh, what a nice job Sal did, honey!" Clearly, her standards were shaken.

"Yeah," I cringed as I raked the curls back with all my fingers, "she did."

I entertained Brad until Daddy arrived home from work. Momma had prepared a simple meal of store-bought, broccoli-cheese soup garnished with popcorn. The conversation was as light as dinner.

After a quick clean up, I asked Daddy if he would watch Brad so Momma and I could slip away to the mall. He nodded, not suspecting a thing. Momma drove. On the way, a red light caught her.

When she braked, I turned to her with a mouthful of hurt. "Momma, why didn't you tell me?"

Long story short. Momma found a job, her first in nearly thirty years, in downtown Minneapolis as a hostess at the courtesy club of a local bank. Her soft skills made her perfect for the position, which bolstered her identity and her courage. She had dropped weight and looked smashing in her pants suits, which concealed her leg braces. Only fashionistas would notice her clompy, black, tie-up shoes.

She wanted more out of her marriage and had badgered Daddy with one question, "Leo, do you love me?" According to Momma, the best he could say was "I need you." With their marriage on alert, she caught the attention of a divorced man who was a frequent visitor to the bank club. Whether it was a slow courtship or a quick trip into her paramour's arms, I don't know. Momma ended up coupling with this man who was a mustached, retired scientist. I have no doubt that she thought she could evangelize her new companion, but instead, he died of cancer shortly after her divorce was final.

I spent months deconstructing the demise of my parent's marriage. I had watched them for years. They rarely touched, but that didn't mean they weren't happy, did it? My assumptions blinded me until my mind cleared for new questions. Why now and not before? Were they sticking it out for their daughters? Were the Bible teachings holding them together? I was confused, embarrassed, and angry, but I kept those feelings buried with my questions. They roiled around like toxins, difficult to digest and impossible to forget.

Daddy and Momma were in Minneapolis for several years before the lock on their marriage busted and led to the divorce that no one saw coming. Momma wanted to be loved and Daddy wanted to be needed and somewhere between the two was a gap wide enough for their wedding rings to fall through. Momma would win the prize of being able to see her four grandchildren grow up. Daddy had already won a disease-free bride, newly widowed with a house in a nice neighborhood and a penchant for eating out.

Daddy met Jane through Grandma Sig. Jane was in Sig's painting class, docented for the Minnesota Historical Society, and was a lecturer at Weight Watchers. What a fine resume for a man in his mid-fifties on the cusp of retirement and looking for a companion. Daddy and Jane married without fanfare and made a whirlwind trip to Texas to show us their rings. They seemed genuinely fond of each other. Ellie and I were young mothers when Daddy put what was left of his household in storage and moved into Jane's two-story on a quiet street, a healthy walk to a lake in one direction and a mall in the other.

Daddy traded in a lifetime of church service and the technicalities of Bible doctrine for a woman without a religious bone in her body. The devout habits that oriented his first marriage were tossed out in a gust of change. Was the church too cruel a reminder of what his Heavenly Father had allowed?

eighteen

Ray and I had settled in the Dallas-Fort Worth area where he was finishing up his Masters, and I was busy mothering Brad, reading all that I could about the quick progression between infant and toddler, observing Brad to make sure he was responsive to all external cues. During that time, I adjusted to the idea of having divorced parents, congratulated my father on his new wife, welcomed my beautiful daughter in a home birth with the help of a midwife, and finished my teaching degree at the ripe age of twenty-nine.

"Took you long enough." Daddy whispered as he side-hugged me in the parking lot after attending my college graduation in the spring of 1987. He had said he wouldn't miss it for the world, and he didn't. Nine-month old Liz was in my arms and Brad stood at my side. Did Daddy have any sense of what my summa cum laude accomplishment had required? I had paid my own way with a Pell Grant, commuted to a school an hour away from home, and earned my credits despite the demands of young motherhood. I wished he had congratulated me with different words, but maybe he was trying to tell me not to put my life on hold for somebody else. I never thought to ask him.

In a rash of good timing, Ray was offered a job in Houston, and I signed my first teaching contract for the Houston school district. We were excited by the idea of moving to a metropolitan area known for its international flair.

Born of bayous and wetlands, Houston had grown into a sprawl of municipalities and neighborhoods that fanned out from its central business district like long spokes on a gigantic wheel. Its lack of zoning had been decried as an obstacle to order, but no zoning had also kept Houston real. The automotive repair shop with the rusty chainlink fence sat on the same block as the finest restaurant in town. Patrons of each co-existed in an agreement that they all belonged. Through floods and hurricanes, Houstonians stuck together. A mosaic of cultures lifted the metropolis into a colorful, delicious, exotic island on the edge of the Deep South. Mixing up good vibes was a talent that served the city well, and it was a good place for Ray and me to try our hands at making it as full-fledged adults.

We bought a house in a mid-century tract home community in the southwest quadrant of the city. The neighborhood of thirty-year-old ranch homes showed wear, but the oaks were stellar. The big yard, the birds, and a sunset view excited us.

Our purchase price was a mere fifty-five thousand dollars because of the recent oil bust. We needed a bump of two-thousand dollars to make our down payment, and Ray had already received some earlier help from his parents for our move, so I asked Daddy for a loan. I was good for the money, I assured him, since I would be teaching soon. He replied without a minute's hesitation, "No."

Surprised and hurt, I didn't have the courage to ask why. "I understand, Daddy." I said in a bald-faced lie. I hadn't asked him for a penny since I had left home. Did he not trust me or was this one more in a line of reminders that I was to be responsible for myself? After that phone call, I swore that I would never ask Daddy for financial help again.

A new twist offered consolation. Momma listened to my frustration and offered the money with only one stipulation. She was moving to Houston. "Could I stay with you all until I get settled?" she propositioned. Momma moved to Houston in a combo-wombo that brought her closer to us and to the Colonel, the doctrinal dogmatist whom she had so admired.

My entrance into teaching bolstered my self-esteem. After five years of being Suzy Homemaker, finishing college, and juggling a scant budget for a family of four, I felt the affirmation of earning a paycheck again, even though half my monthly salary was going for preschool and daycare. Thankfully,

Brad would start first grade soon. Conversely, Ray was having a crisis of confidence and suffering from what I now understand was depression. We managed the kids just fine, but in our time alone, our ability to communicate was failing. The marriage, which had been fracturing since my parents' divorce, fell apart with no possible repair. I had an affair. Ray sunk deeper into darkness. I asked him to move out, and he did.

The subsequent adjustments were many, as so many families know. My parents were saddened, but what could they say? On most weekends, the kids stayed with Ray. We had committed to co-parenting for the long haul. This was a concept foreign to my father. He had broken off relations with Momma as soon as the ink dried on their divorce papers. He would never speak to her again, which was an aspect of our family dynamic that was hard to explain to the children.

My role shifted to single mom, or as I liked to think of myself, head of household. That was a promotion. I rose to meet my responsibilities as consistently as I could. I wasn't perfect. I fed my children chicken nuggets, fast food burgers, and take-out pizza. On my menus, ketchup was definitely a vegetable.[40] I packed the kids' lunches with deli meat swimming in additives. Dessert was always available, albeit Little Debbies, the cheapest of the nutritionless offerings on the cookie aisle. Easy, cheap, and clean was my motto. *(Sorry, kids.)*

After dinner on weeknights, we watched *The Simpsons*, something Ellie refused to allow her daughter and son to do. While the kids laughed at the slapstick humor, I chuckled at the social commentary that slipped over their heads. The older they grew, the more cerebral they learned the show to be. We each had our favorite characters. I split my vote between Lisa and Marge. Liz liked Dr. Nick. Brad was a Homer fan. Even now, "Separate Vocations," "The Springfield Files," and "El Viaje Misterioso de Neustro Jomer" remain some of our favorite episodes. How did we get from *Mr. Rogers* to *The Simpsons*? All I can say is, both were ripe for their time.

As Liz and Brad grew older, we also tuned in to *Homicide: Life on the Street*[41]

---

[40] Proposals during the Reagan administration suggested that ketchup be counted as a vegetable in school meals.
[41] An American police procedural television series that ran for seven seasons on NBC from 1993 to 1999

on Friday nights and rarely missed an episode. The investigative nature of the storylines reawakened my curiosity about Daddy's career. I watched for clues about the day-to-day experience of the detectives and appreciated the racial diversity, writing, and cast. Our entertainment hours let me develop my own version of Momness. I could lighten up, be less sacrosant, more vulnerable during scenes that delivered an emotional punch. I had seldom seen my parents unguarded, and it felt good to share time with the kids around edgy humor and complex questions that didn't have easy answers.

nineteen

I didn't have complete confidence in my parenting skills. I needed a support system, a village. I hadn't had a village for a very long time. I had been treading water in shifting currents and had only my stick-to-it-tiveness to thank for making it this far. Since the divorce, I had stumbled into unhealthy relationships. One salty encounter had me convinced that I could no longer afford poor judgment. I needed to get back on the straight and narrow. I also couldn't expect the television to be the only influence in my children's lives. Join a church, my logic told me. That's what people do.

Since Momma's move to Houston, she had generously stepped into the roles of chauffeur and babysitter, allowing Brad and Liz to get a break from me every now and then and to be in the cuddly arms of their cheerful Gram. Her willingness to watch the kids allowed me to take on a second job and start my Master's. If her divorce from Daddy had a silver lining, that was it. She had joined the Colonel's church and dropped multiple hints about what a good place it would be for me and the kiddos. *What could it hurt*, I wondered. Momma's presence in our lives had been a saving grace. We could give it a try.

When I stepped onto the asphalt in the parking lot of the church made famous by the Colonel, I took Momma's arm and the kids trailed behind me in compliant resistance. Why wasn't I able to put myself in their shoes? What a hypocrite I was! I had not yet found the higher power that I had promised to find when I was girl of thirteen. How could I return to the religious fundamentalism that had caused my suffering in the first place? Isn't insanity defined as doing the same thing over and over again expecting a different result?

One thing the church was good at was offering forgiveness. That concept alone had reeled in many desperate wretches over millennia, strengthening the pull toward "the fisher of men." All those lost souls wanted a clean slate, and I was one of them. In my single-mindedness, I was determined to prove myself to be a good girl, once and for all. What moved me to take such drastic action? The twin devastators of so many souls, guilt and shame.

There Momma and I were, two divorced women, walking into the sanctuary of the proprietor of Right Man/Right Woman with two new recruits, whom I was dragging along. We attended Bible class multiple times a week, two classes on Sundays and two week nights. Each time slot offered a different topic, all directed by the Colonel's passions to interpret the scriptures through his paternalistic, militaristic, homophobic viewpoint. The Colonel was 80 years old by then, but just as imposing. I curtseyed to his proclamations and caught what breadcrumbs I could to pacify myself.

I buried myself in doctrinal certainties and rigid rules, submitting to a lord and master. I became addicted to "the truth of the Word." I took notes like a professional and peered at the Colonel's face like a groupie. If my mind wandered, I pinched my thighs and told myself to do better, try harder. On some nights, my tears would inexplicably flow in an uncontrollable stream that I could not conceal, blurring my vision and dissolving my mascara so I looked like Tammy Faye.[42] I steadied my gaze on my notebook on those nights, hoping no one would notice. My deepest emotions seemed to be begging for attention, but I wasn't ready to heed their call.

I joined the church and after a year or so began teaching Sunday night Bible class for the fifth graders, including Liz. Brad was already in the teen group, which was taught by the ramrod-postured son of the Colonel. Women weren't trusted to teach children over the age of twelve.

---

[42] Tammy Faye [Bakker] Messner was a Christian television personality who gained notice on *The PTL* [Praise the Lord] *Club*. When she cried, her tears devastated her heavy eye makeup.

twenty

When the kids were well into elementary school, I transferred from a middle school job with a commute to the neighborhood high school a couple blocks away. The kids could each ride a school bus to their respective schools, and I could be home to see them off and greet them when they returned home again.

The best snapshot I can offer of the high school to which I transferred is that the freshmen class weighed in at over nine hundred students, but fewer than two hundred saw it through to graduation. The poverty was blatant, but the students were in need of just as much attention and support as students anywhere.

I moved into my windowless classroom ready to learn the ropes of high school teaching, motivated by the challenge of ninth grade English. Teaching to the state test, a must in Texas, stole some of my joy, but not all of it. Once the year was underway and survival seemed possible, I started wearing a genuine smile, but even with the addition of church-going, something was missing. Nearing forty, I forecast a lonely future ahead. My life was absent of a sense of belonging, a feeling of being known. I hadn't had a heart-to-heart friend since my freshman year of college.

One morning, the French teacher, who had a classroom near me, approached with a tried and true Texas "Howdy!" that bounced all the way to the tips of her blond ponytail and dangled from her turquoise earrings. I had already noticed in faculty meetings that she possessed a Southern accent that put mine to shame. I had also noted that her fashionable hipness beat my sense of style by a mile. "Wanna have lunch?" she asked. An angel on my shoulder told me to say yes.

Patrice and I began to share occasional meals. We'd meet in her classroom, decked out with lamps and pillows and posters of Paris and the French countryside. Our twenty-minute lunches were like the vacation I had needed for a long, long time. Soon we were lunching daily. I learned that she had moved to Houston to support a dear high school friend diagnosed with AIDS. Patrice sponsored the International Club and had organized a school trip to France and raised 22K for students in the Title I school where she had taught in where else but Jackson, Mississippi. Our connections flowered.

I began to confide in her my deepest longings and fears: my financial worries, extended family concerns, and most surprisingly, a crush I had on another English teacher. I even told her about the Colonel's church. Our friendship deepened, and I began to feel the way I had felt reading Anne's diary when I was a girl. Trust grew between us, and I felt the power of my own honest words traveling to a listening ear.

We talked of the complications of love. Patrice was divorced and identified as bisexual. About my crush, she cautioned me to "Be careful." My receptivity to that advice strengthened me against heartache. When my sexuality became a topic of conversation, little by little, I unearthed myself.

I indulged in stories about Jade that had us both either in stitches or tears. "She fired up something inside me," I confessed to Patrice. Sharing stories felt so good, so clean and right.

"Sharon, are you a lesbian?" Patrice asked one weekend when we had driven to a Galveston beach with Pookie, her dog.

We had been walking the shoreline barefoot, and I turned toward the surf before I answered. "Maybe." Was I ready to consider the whole of who I might be? "Maybe I am."

In time, Patrice introduced me to Yvonne, a deep-voiced philosophy teacher, who drew out her seven-syllable words in deep yawns as she drew on imaginary cigarettes. She was an arrogant feminist with attitude. I hung on her every lesbian word even though she wasn't kind enough to be my type.

One Saturday night in January, we three found ourselves around the kitchen table in Patrice's inviting garage apartment. As a fragrant stir fry of onions, squash, and peppers sizzled on the gas stove, the subject of spring break broke through the thunder of school talk.

"Brad and Liz will be with their dad. I'll be a free bird!" My wine glass rose above the table as I begged a toast.

"Here! Here!" Yvonne shouted in throaty agreement, clinking my glass with hers.

"Woohoo!" Patrice added with a clink of her own. She promptly excused herself and brought back a map, a good omen. Maps had delivered me to new vistas since I saw my first one around the table in Minneapolis when I was a child. I couldn't imagine who I would be without them.

Before the night was over we had conjured a trip to Canyon de Chelly, which branches eastwards from Chinle, Arizona, into the Defiance Plateau. As I drove home, memories of childhood roadtrips clouded the windshield. I'd have to tell Daddy that I was heading west for an adventure. "Oh, really?" he would say. "You and who?"

Patrice, Yvonne, and I landed in Albuquerque and drove to the Navajo lodge at Canyon de Chelley. We determined our schedule for visiting the Anasazi cliff dwellings, exploring the rock art, and establishing the best stargazing sites. A Navajo guide named Ernest led us into the canyon one evening when the night sky boasted not only the Hale-Bopp comet,[43] but a partial eclipse and meteor shower, which had been part of our reason for coming.

As we planted ourselves in the foot of the canyon, with the brilliant sky show above, Ernest's flute warbled a reverent acknowledgement of the sacredness of the earth and sky. Was it the moonlight or the cool desert air or the shadows that fell from the canyon walls? All I knew was that I felt that the heavens and carved earth had given me something to believe in, and I was happy. What was it that Anne had said? *"The best remedy for those who are afraid, lonely or unhappy is to go outside, somewhere where they can be quiet, alone with the heavens, nature and God. Because only then does one feel that all is*

---

[43] Comet Hale-Bopp (1997) was perhaps the brightest, most widely observed sighting of the 20th century.

as it should be and that God wishes to see people happy, amidst the simple beauty of nature."

As we climbed out of the canyon, the moon was in shadow and the stars appeared like guests at a surprise party in the sky's honor. I had lived without celestial bliss for far too long.

The next day, we traveled to more ruins, then on to Spider Rock and the twin 800-foot towers of sandstone that rise from the canyon floor. We perched like saplings on a remote ledge to take it all in. A raven glided past at eye level. Magical.

"Do you mind if I sing?" I asked my canyonmates.

"Sing on, baby!" Patrice coaxed me, always up for a song. Yvonne nodded, her eyes fixed on the far horizon. What came from deep inside was a hymn, a favorite of both Momma and Daddy.

My voice emptied into the expanse and evaporated into the blue as the visible cloak of time swept from horizon to horizon. *"Great is Thy faithfulness, O God my Father...*WAIT! Let me start again....*Great is thy faithfulness, O Earth my Mother..."* I turned to Patrice. She nodded, encouraging me. *"There is no shadow of turning with Thee....thou changest not thy compassions they fail not, as thou hast been thou forever wilt be."* A rush of canyon air rose into my nostrils and a smile bloomed. "That felt SO DAMN GOOD!" I admitted, laughing like a child. The other two women laughed with me and our echoes returned to us in a harmony of joy. An inkling of the power that held me to Anne and Anne to eternity wrapped me in its arms. We existed together in the expanse of this beauty, this unbounded love.

∞

twenty-one

The year was 1999 and attention was focused on the fears and hopes of a new century, from Y2K to the possibilities for equity and justice for an ever-growing list of the under-represented.

I walked with the kids, now teenagers, from the parking lot toward our first family picnic at the Houston prep school where I had accepted a teaching position. The faculty event capped off a week of inservices before the start of school. As we moved closer to the gathering crowd, I spotted a woman sitting in a coaching position, hands clasped between open knees, trunk forward, head tilted toward the slight man beside her on the concrete bench under an open stairwell. *I wonder who she is?* I thought. My newborn gaydar[44] pinged.

"Come on, kids, let's hit the buffet line," I strategized. We wove our way toward the smell of grilling chicken as Brad and Liz traipsed behind me, their flip-flopped feet dragging. I spied young children, all White, on the nearby pristine playground. Was it my imagination or were they outfitted for a fashion magazine layout? I was entering a world that I had already sensed was a million miles away from the schools where I had been teaching in Houston's public system.

Over an eleven-year stretch, I had worked at five different public schools, always striving for better: better course loads, better administrators, better community support. My network expanded as I hopped from school to school, and one of my dear colleagues, a librarian, had, when she learned of an opening at the elite private school, encouraged me. "You must apply! You'd be perfect for it." her phone message exclaimed. Could I support my

---

[44] a colloquialism referring to the intuitive ability of a person to assess others' sexual orientations

family on a private school teacher's salary? I had my doubts.

The administrators who interviewed me assured me I could and hired me despite my public school education, lack of pedigree, and a home address that indicated a neighborhood on the sketchy southwest side.

As my heart vibrated to the beat of the homogeneous drum corps marching our way in their Rebel gear, I wondered what I had gotten myself into. Rebels? Not again!

My head turned back toward the fair face of the woman on the bench under the stairwell. She was still in deep conversation. *I need to get to know her*, I thought, feeling a clean, clear attraction.

"Look, Mom, fajitas!" Brad whispered. Liz chimed in, "And check out the huge bowl of guacamole!" Suddenly the kids were dragging me along to the red and white tablecloths where the catering staff waited with serving spoons in hand. *This just might work*, I thought.

That night, I learned Trish's name and that she was the Upper School Counselor and the junior varsity basketball coach and had moved from the East the year before. I introduced her to the kids as we toured the new fine arts auditorium with a large group. Members of the faculty grabbed Trish away for one conversation after another. After a final stop at the dessert table, the kids and I walked over to have a look at my classroom. I didn't see Trish again until weeks later.

In the meantime, I was schooled on the environment I had entered. Money oozed from the pores of the seventh graders whom I taught and advised. Special lunches were arranged by mothers around the country gardens of their sprawling estates, girls my daughter's age had their eyebrows waxed, every foot wore the brightest and best of sneakers, dozens of bar mitzvahs and bat mitzvahs complicated the due dates for projects and tests, and I learned in one brief moment what not to use as a writing prompt: *What I Did on Summer Vacation*. One innocent youth responded in her opening sentence that "My family visited our seventh continent this summer!" Her excitement was only exceeded by my mortification. Over time, I created alternatives that drew less on the fantastical adventures of the haves and more on the ideas of empathy and compassion.

One morning, I woke up with the urge to make contact with Trish. Sitting in my favorite corner of the sofa with my cup of coffee in the predawn hours, I looked through my shoebox of collected cards and spotted one I had nabbed in one of my buying sprees. The card's cover showcased the word *Intention* in a bold, large font calligraphy of dark blues and silvers. The inside was blank. *Perfect*, I thought.

I scribbled a draft message in the front flap of my daily planner. I wanted to be straightforward and avoid innuendo. *Hoping we can grab a bite or catch a movie sometime soon. Take it easy! Sharon.* I transferred the message to the card like I was doing it for a grade then added my phone number and personal email.

During my afternoon conference period, I walked past the stairwell where I had first spotted Trish and on through the tunnel that connected the south and north campuses. I pretended to know exactly where I was going.

"Can I help you with something?" the main office receptionist, an aging woman who still dyed her hair a sandy brown, asked with a concern born more of curiosity than service. She might have been sizing me up, estimating my height, taller than most, and noting my hip wobble.

"No, thanks," I replied, keeping the envelope inside my patchwork vest, secured by the glue of my forearm. As if on cue, Trish's name plate appeared outside an office door that stood open. I strode inside without a stumble, left the card on the corner of her desk, and retraced my steps without ever touching the ground. I'm sure the receptionist discovered the card well before Trish did.

The way she tells it, Trish showed the card to two of her trusted colleagues in the P.E. department. "I don't have time for another straight friendship," she confided to them.

"Let's look at her bio," the clever girl's basketball coach suggested. The faculty section of the school directory turned out to offer a tipping point in my favor. I had graduated from a women's university so they extrapolated that I might not be a complete waste of time. They also noted that I wore sensible shoes.

twenty-two

After a few casual dates, a romance blossomed. Trish and I found so much common ground. Several months of serious dating included lots of time learning each other's histories, comforts, and dreams. When the kids were at Ray's on the weekends, Trish's apartment became our love nest. She joined the kids and me in Sharpstown for dinner one evening a week. Still, I was cautious where Brad and Liz were concerned. I had no idea how any of us would handle a full-flowering of this relationship. Complications would be plenty, especially with family. My identity had been set. To them, I was a single mom, divorced for ten years. And I was still teaching Bible classes at one of the most conservative churches in the city.

Momma and I sat on the couch side by side, and I looked straight ahead through the patio door to the live oak as I talked on and on using every justification I could to make the news that I was, indeed, a lesbian, less painful. Her dimples vanished. She snapped her head and met me eye to eye. "It's against scripture, little girl!" she reminded me.

I didn't want to get into a Bible fight, so I backed off. "Sorry, Mom. But remember, I'm a grown woman, not a little girl." She sat frozen beside me. Momma and I had weathered many a battle together, and we would survive this one, I hoped.

"So, Jade?" Momma asked. She picked at a fuzzball on her sweater.

"Yes, Jade." I answered. So Momma remembered. My heart swelled with an ache at the memory of Jade. Momma shook her head in silence and yanked the fuzzball hard.

I had already received a message of disgust from my father. I had mailed a long letter in triplicate to Momma, Daddy, and Ellie.[45] His response read like a long shoulder-shaking session. He expressed visceral disbelief that an intelligent woman like me would *"make a decision so contrary to all teachings and good sense...If you were stupid, I could charge this off to that, but you are not stupid."* His fatherly advice was to *"reconsider the many ramifications of this decision and to be the prodigal daughter."*[46] He made his point years later in the legalities of his will. His wife and my sister were listed as executors, I was not. Daddy had pegged me as an untrustworthy deviant, something I wouldn't discover for a long, long time.

Any open-mindedness on Daddy's part was a casualty of the era of J. Edgar Hoover, a famously homophobic creature. Gays were seen as a national security threat.[47] Daddy was not interested in exploring the possibility that all those men and women were sons and daughters, too. But we are, aren't we?

Ellie disassociated from me, Trish, and my children for several years as a result. She did not want me to contact her and returned birthday cards and photographs, some unopened. Whatever softened her to include our family again in a holiday gathering, I will never know. In a mysterious change of heart, she welcomed me back as a sister although she never explained why. We met in the gap between her life and mine with a tricky mix of affection and caution.

After a few weeks of dating Trish, I quit the church. My mother was devastated. The kids were overjoyed. I was growing up. "Took you long enough," I couldn't help but tell myself, echoing Daddy's comments upon my tardy college graduation. The late-bloomer strikes again.

That summer, Trish and I planned a ten-day vacation together during the short window when Brad and Liz would be with Ray's family. We checked

---

[45] See the letter on sharonhopefabriz.com on the *Circling Toward Home* page.
[46] Reference to a parable of Jesus about a son who has left his family with full disapproval and who returns home feeling sorry for what he has done
[47] Charles, Douglas M., *Hoover's War on Gays: Exposing the F.B.I.s "Sex Deviates" Program* (2015)

our unwieldy duffles all the way to San Francisco and picked up a rental for a week of car camping up the northern California coast. We were ready to test the ground rules we had written together. Be honest. Be kind. Be true.

The trip to California became a wellspring of discovery and set us on a path of adventure. When we arrived home, it was painful for us to be in separate homes, to wake up without the pleasure of sharing coffee together, a ritual we've held on to now for more than twenty years.

Autumn rolled around and with it the presidential election of 2000. Bush and Kerry supporters snarled at each other, and the staunchest on each side were livid with Nader for crashing the electoral party. A week or so before the election, Ralph Nader spoke during a televised Green Party rally. That Sunday afternoon, Brad and Liz watched with interest, their own budding political identities anxious to chew on any offerings more palatable than the beastly regurgitations of elephants and donkeys. When I heard the cheers for Nader wane and a political ad blaring, I called the kids back to my bedroom, a room where we had huddled from storms, a room where when sick we recovered, a room of quiet and calm.

"Come on up. Sit with me," I patted the mattress hard. "How was the speech?"

Uh, okay, the silent nods suggested. Already I could tell that my invitation had perked their antennae. *What is going on*, their adolescent eyes begged.

This wasn't about how they hadn't been helping enough with the chores. "Well," I started, feeling the tightening in my stomach, "you both know how much I've enjoyed Trish's company lately, right?" That was the easy part. From the first brownie-baking afternoon several months before to the weekly meals since, Trish's presence in our lives was commonplace to them by now. Grasping for the most honest of the words that tumbled around in my head, I simply said, "I love her."

I reached for their hands, needing the certainty of touch. And then for the clarity we all needed I said something like "I hate to spring this on you, but your mom is a lesbian." Their blank faces held my gaze as I continued, "And I want to talk about it. I want to tell you my story." Both nodded lightly like a disconcerting mystery was about to unfold.

As we sat close, I whispered my truth that Sunday afternoon. "I had a girlfriend in high school. Her name was Jade. I was crazy about her...." I told my story of heartbreak. I admitted that my sexual orientation had been submerged for decades, that I hadn't given it much thought. I had woken up to it in a gradual surprise.

"I am most thankful that my path led me to your dad because we gave life to each of you. Nothing in the world is more important to me than your health, safety, and happiness. That will never change. I love you." Their eyes were intent, their silence careful. We cried a little and hugged a lot, and I proposed an answer to the big "What now?"

The entire situation must have been hard for them. Our reliable three-person family had been all we had known for most of their lifetimes. Yes, they had their dad and grandparents and aunts and cousins, but mostly we three had each other. I loved being a mother, their mother. I also recognized that being true to my own sense of self was something that I hoped would encourage them to follow suit.

Life moved quickly after that afternoon. Trish gave up her lease and moved in piece by piece until before long she was a full-fledged resident, cat included. New challenges began with the blending of households, and each of us managed ourselves the best we could. It wasn't always pretty, but we tried hard to make the new arrangement work. Lessons were botched and corrected along the way. In a few short years, both Brad and Liz graduated from high school and left Houston for their own adventures. They both had endured my divorce, fundamentalist church-going, and my coming out, along with growing pains of their own. Had my arrested development harmed them? I needed to let those worries go. My deep desire to show them that I could have a healthy, loving, committed relationship was coming into view.

twenty-three

Despite the harsh realities of bias against gay couples by family and the State of Texas, Trish and I were able to maintain professionalism at our prep school during the first fourteen years of the new century without bringing attention to ourselves. The national conversation about gay rights would not reach a fever pitch for a few years yet. We knew we could not afford any errors in judgment and performed at 150% to ensure our employment status. That reality is common to the marginalized, those who must work harder to prove themselves, secure their positions, be tolerated by those who sign the paycheck.

Luckily, my principal was a great listener. I confided in him about my home life, and he responded with attention and care. In part because my superior was a visible ally, a Sharon and Trish fan club developed, and our circle of friends expanded among the faculty, despite the school's general blindness to our relationship.

Our school identities wrapped around us like well-worn scarves, as familiar to us as our own habits and personal routines. Yes, we still struggled with the patriarchal structures, the embedded classism, and the White privilege. Trish led efforts to educate the administration and faculty to issues of equity and diversity while I, with a Black colleague and dear friend, co-sponsored a middle school club which we called Under One Nation, a place for students to hear and share stories of difference in the safety of an environment where all were welcome. We also benefited from the school's wealth in terms of its physical plant, benefits package, annual raises, all the way down to the generous gifts received from the families whose children we taught. I had gone from the self-consciousness of being a "have" among the public school students I taught to feeling self-conscious for the older model car I drove and the B-grade fashions I wore. I laughed with full appreciation at the faculty jokes about steering clear of the senior parking lot and its flashy reminders of our status as servants of the rich. I drove the six miles home aware that with every mile the environment changed from moneyed to struggling.

The first decade of our relationship almost ended without a hitch. Developments on the LGBTQ front were promising. In 2009, Annise Parker was elected mayor of Houston and became the first openly lesbian mayor of a major city in Texas. The next year, the U.S. Senate voted to repeal the U.S. military's "Don't Ask, Don't Tell" policy, allowing gays and lesbians to serve openly. Aside from work and Trish's coaching, we busied ourselves with remodeling projects, summertime development of a rural property in Colorado, and family travel, including trips to her generous and welcoming sister and brothers in Virginia.

I joined a writing group and involved myself with The Center for Courage and Renewal[48] and developed a number of friendships with members of my circle of trust in Washington State, where I attended seasonal retreats. I also befriended a small group of women in Houston who mirrored my soul. My peeps loved me for who I was and modeled courage, compassion, and creativity to keep me blooming. They continue to inspire me to embrace the fierce feminism in my bones. I can't imagine my life without the benefit of the circles of supportive women like the ones I sought and found. Kinships both temporal and long-lasting strengthened my ability to meet the world's pain and my own. In my heart, they all have a seat at our community table, laden with friendship and love.

---

[48] The Center for Courage & Renewal is a nonprofit organization founded in 1997 by author, activist, and educator Parker J. Palmer. The website defines CC&R as grounded in a social technology of time-tested principles and practices for helping people "rejoin soul and role."

During our ninth year together, Trish was diagnosed with non-Hodgkins lymphoma. The news sent shockwaves through us and our families, and we joined the millions who have felt the jolt of a cancer diagnosis. Trish continued to work through the entire chemo regimen, outfitting herself with colorful bandanas and putting her illness offstage as she fulfilled her professional role with a focus that never waivered. It helped that her medical insurance covered a freakishly expensive anti-nausea medication that many health care plans did not. Trish and I began to see up close and personal the uneven delivery of care in the U.S. health system. That it worked in her favor caused an ambivalence in me that was hard to explain. Trish told stories of how tiered care was apparent in her observations of the situations of other patients in the chemo treatment room. Why? I asked myself. I considered Daddy's claim that "life isn't fair." As I looked back over all of the things that he had claimed were unfair, I saw a pattern. Upon closer examination, human decisions based in profit margins and greed were often at the root. For-profit and even not-for-profit U.S. healthcare systems were bound to maximize the wealth of the few, and the general consensus seemed to be that an overpriced, inequitable system was the American way.[49]

The next five years continued without major incident. We toasted Trish's good health on yearly anniversaries and put the cancer worries behind us. In January of 2014, Trish noticed that the upper thigh where one of her primary tumors had developed was beginning to swell. Trish's remission ended, ripping us both to the bone.

Her oncologist recommended that she transfer to M.D. Anderson Cancer Center. Her new team recommended a stem cell transplant. The largest stem cell transplant operation in the world was a mere fifteen-minute drive from our house. I knew nothing of such possibilities and was wary, but I trusted Trish. She decided to go for it. Despite the infancy of the harrowing procedure, early reviews lauded the approach. We were hopeful.

As before, she wanted to protect her privacy. No big announcements, just a discreet accommodation for her chemo schedule. She was bound and determined to continue to teach her social/emotional learning classes and

---

[49] In 2018, 62 CEOs of health-care companies made a combined total of $1.1 billion in compensation.

perform her counseling duties. When her treatments began in early spring, she pulled out her collection of bandanas and reasserted her right to privacy, the thing she valued most. The year before, we had adopted a dog, and Mocha was there with us to buffer the blows of all that awaited.

Once the extended, time-consuming procedure began, *How's Trish?* became a question that I heard from sincere sources and downright nosy ones. I created a group email called Trish Update and composed the messages with a range of people in mind, from liberal pals to conservative family. I walked a tightrope that wouldn't stop swaying. Trish wanted privacy but colleagues, friends, and family wanted to show their care. The stress of being the conduit tired me. I found myself looking in the mirror and reminding myself that this was what it meant to be with someone in sickness. We weren't married, still a legal impossibility in Texas, but we were in this relationship for the long haul. I wanted to excel at my role like so many caregivers do.

Once the chemo ended, Trish was to be hospitalized so that the harvesting of healthy stem cells could begin. The transplant was scheduled for July so our usual summer move to our land in Colorado would be cut short between the end of Trish's chemo and her hospital admission.

Ten years before, on the advice of my dear friend Patrice, who had since moved to Denver, Trish and I purchased two adjoining lots totaling eleven acres in the foothills of the Sangre de Cristo range of southern Colorado. Our acreage offered 360 degree views and became a refuge that took us off-grid and taught us a whole new set of survival skills. We made the sixteen-hour trek as often as was practical—in the best years, we went three times, with a six-week stretch in the summer. We had a vintage trailer hauled to the property early on and then drafted plans for a 600 square-foot cabin wired for solar power, We created a place to reorient ourselves and fell hook, line, and sinker for our beloved Circle Dance Ranch.

Getting to the cabin for a brief stay prior to the stem cell transfer was the plan. The end of the spring semester couldn't come fast enough. For me, the last required day for teachers never failed to be a bittersweet departure. I had my own end-of-school ritual that required a few minutes alone in my middle school classroom. I took a slow walk along each wall, around the tables and chairs, eyeing the last bags of garbage by the door, the mountain of recycling. To me, nothing felt more abandoned than an emptied classroom at the end of the school year. Likely, it reminded me of all the empty rooms that were left behind in the many moves of childhood. What existed of a classroom's history? What rippled outward into the students' lives from the progress accomplished in that space? I heard echoes of the chill-bump times when one child said to another "That's deep." I already knew that the seeds planted in a thirteen-year-old heart can remain there for a lifetime, the way Anne Frank's diary had taken root in me.

I tugged at the last two bags of supplies that would live in our garage until my August return. Hooking their handles over my shoulder, I managed to wedge my hearty ivy in the crook of my other arm. I had an appointment for a pedicure at the Bliss Spa so my toes could be popping in my favorite summer sandals. Trish had given me a gift card for my April birthday, my fifty-sixth, and I had strategized that the last day of school was the perfect time to use it.

Mine was one of the last cars left in the teachers' parking lot and was baking after a day of harsh Texas sun. I rolled down all the windows to release the steam, then secured the plant on the passenger side, cranked on the air, threw on my sunglasses, and shifted into reverse.

The spa was in the opposite direction of home and took me past the north campus on up through the chichi neighborhoods where many of my students lived. Hot pink crepe myrtles jeweled the yards, and border gardens of bold perennials laced the abodes of the old money landowners.

Just as I approached a speed bump along the north campus, my phone rang. A favorite photo of Trish glowed from the screen. I switched to speaker, excited to report my location.

"Hi, honey! I'm just around the corner, heading to the spa. What's up?" I said with the cheer that only the last official day of the school year can bring.

A flatline response followed. "You mean what's down. I just got canned."

The words didn't make sense, and my ability to answer was reduced to a confused, "What?"

"He-who-shall-not-be-named stood at the door and told me that my services were no longer needed. The school is moving in another direction, he said." I thought about the recent change in administration, the new business model, the recent rash of retirements and new hires. Was Trish the latest casualty?

I slowed to a crawl, glad to be the only car on the street. Another speed bump appeared, and I slid over it like a slug. My hands gripped the wheel. "You've got to be kidding. I don't get it." I did get it, but I wasn't going to say so. Not right now. Trish didn't fit the new business model. She was the kind of woman who was regularly called, "sir," and opted for sneakers. Lipstick? Never! She'd been wearing bandanas to cover her bald head because of the months of chemo required before the stem cell transplant. Her style wasn't the brand the school was now hawking. Beyond that, as high school counselor, she had been the vessel to hold faculty grievances and concerns regarding unpalatable administrative actions for the past several years.

"I have to turn in my computer and empty my desk by the end of the day. That's all I know." She sounded defeated. "I've been in here with my door closed trying to decide when to call you." A deep inhale followed. "I'll see you at home."

"Honey! Wait! Are you okay?" A spiny sense of worry kicked in. Trish's identity flowed from her professional role. Her temperate ways, generous listening, and astute advice were respected in every division of the school. She was a champion for diversity and inclusivity not only on our campus but in the community and in national efforts. She was a victim of the very bias she had fought so hard against.

"I'll be fine. Go get your pedi." She sounded mechanical, like a script had been written that she needed to follow.

"My god, babe." I braked suddenly when the approaching light turned red. "I love you."

"Let's get off the phone, okay?" her voice wilted. "I love you, too." We said our goodbyes, and I kept driving, wishing for once that I had an automatic transmission. The day had me shifting too many gears. I rammed the car into second and weaved into the other lane. *Get a-hold of yourself, young lady*, I scolded myself, followed quickly by an audible *Dear Lord. What the hell?*

I could hardly believe what I was doing as wheeled into a parking spot at the spa. I opened the door to the mellow environment designed to bring stress down a notch. A burst of lavender and lemon swept over me as a sleek, dark-haired woman approached. I gave my name, and she showed me to a massage chair.

"How are you doing today?" she asked, interrupting an ambient piano sonata that soothed the air.

"To be honest, I'm not much in the mood to talk." I confessed as I unbuckled my sandal straps. My reply surprised even me, but unconsciously I must have known that I couldn't chat my way into normalcy. Uncertainty had been a daily companion since the return of Trish's cancer. Now another flare had exploded. I sat captive and silent as the technician kept her head low and her eyes focused on the brittle nails before she could add the Faraway Blue I had chosen without thinking.

On the drive home, I understood what Trish's dismissal required of me. That night I wrote a letter to my boss and friend. I would fulfill next year's contract, but my upcoming fifteenth year would be my last at the school that had, until now, provided the most gratifying professional growth opportunities of my career. I didn't digest the full impact of my decision until much later, but the decision remained a watershed moment for me. I chose my relationship over my job. I could do that, and I did.

Ahead of me was a painful school year that I hadn't yet begun to imagine, and the summer would not provide much respite. I would need to call on my deepest resources to meet the days ahead. Thank goodness Grandma Sig had taught me a lyric, one that softened the edges of the sharp corners waiting. As the ground vanished beneath my feet, I found comfort in the song—*que sera sera, what will be will be.*

twenty-four

Our pilgrimage to the cabin took us northwest beyond Wichita Falls and on through Amarillo, into the northeast corner of New Mexico toward the happy turn westward from I-25 at Walsenburg, Colorado. Getting back to cabin time meant taking care of ourselves in the most fundamental of ways. Daylight guided our schedule. Washing a day's worth of dishes and pans in a half-gallon of water became a test of ingenuity and a mindfulness practice. Lugging the five-gallon buckets from the compost toilet to the humanure field for emptying did, too. Contending with mice and other critters was a whole new learning curve, complete with ethical dilemmas.

Every experience seemed layered in metaphor, and cabin time allowed me to process the tasks of daily living as the best teachers around.

I tried to do the math one day as I strode up the dirt road alone. On how many hikes had my footprints molded the sand, kicked the pebbles, splattered the mud? As I made that day's trek up the slow incline to the more demanding slopes and finally to rewarding views of New Mexico mesas to the south, Mount Blanca to the north, the Sangre de Cristos to the east, and the San Luis Valley to the west, I concluded that the total didn't matter. The only hike that mattered was the hike of the moment. The only crisp air, this crisp air. The only jeweled sky, the one in view.

With the rising earth, pinion groves, and dome of blue my company, I incarnated Mary Oliver's advice and "let the soft animal" that is me "love what it loves." I reduced myself and the entire world to each single step, the solid earth, the blessed present.

Near the all-too-brief vacation week's end and with Trish's transplant on the horizon, we agreed that a night spent under the stars before our return was a must. We prepared the bed of the truck with the air mattress, a quilt pile, and pillows plenty. Trish and I crawled into the truck bed near dusk, wearing headlamps and toting books. We read until our eyes were tired of words as twilight bowed to night.

As we lay in silence, the stars emerged, practiced as ever, and shared their magic in what is easily the encore of all nature's shows. I bathed in the velvet heavens: star river, a chorus of rising planets and shooting meteors, animated satellites, la luna grande, but mostly space emptying into space emptying into space emptying into me, setting off soul sparks. The star dance or moon jam or whatever you name it held for me a most elemental lesson, one I could carry in my mind's sky no matter my altitude. Simply put: Light lives on.

We drove back to Houston aware of the unknowns waiting: Trish's stem cell transplant and anticipated recovery, my year of teaching under duress, and my job search, which we had decided would be limited to western states, closer to where both Brad and Liz had relocated. With their assurances that Texas was not a place that they wanted to live their adult lives, I felt free to sell the house and leave the state where I had lived for nearly forty years, aside from a couple years of Naval transfers with my ex-husband, Ray.

I survived the year that demanded I see Trish at death's door while I applied for out-of-state jobs, flying to hiring events and interviews, and managing my current position. I wasn't prepared for the anxiety caused by frequent occasions that had me in close proximity to the head honcho who had fired Trish, and I hadn't expected the perplexed looks I received from some colleagues. Why was Trish let go? they seemed to say.

Besides taking Mocha on long walks to clear my head, one of the wisest things I did for myself over those months to manage my stress was to have regular sessions with an attentive, wise creativity coach, Cyncie, who counseled me to meet my reality with artful responses. She assured me that "the antidote is always nearby."

At a Colorado thrift store, I discovered an old wooden window containing five oblong panes, oozing with creative potential. I hauled it home and wedged it in the garage, ignoring the prized possession for months on end. During the weeks when Trish was in the hospital, the window project became both pastime and passion. I delved into my spiritual journey through painting, collage, assemblage, and poetry. I wrote an intention in gold ink on the panes: *forget wanting (this or that) / embrace everything / gather - hold - wonder / open your window / climb through (heart first) / to freedom (to yes)*. The pleasing result helped me see the road I had traveled in a whole new way. The window was first in a line of creative acts that befriended and stabilized me that difficult year.

I also took to videotaping footage of myself, of Houston, of Trish, over the course of those months and spent hours editing the videos, creating a movie, adding music and narration, all in an attempt to give myself a self-possessed version of a story I could follow.

With Cyncie's guidance, I started writing a novel. Liv, the adolescent protagonist, was a fish out of water, new girl on the block, trying to manage changes she couldn't control. Once Trish was home resting for weeks on end, allowing her body to renew itself, the story offered space for both obsession and confession. I poured into its pages what remained of my adolescent angst, my anger at systemic racism, my familial struggles, and the questions about heaven and hell that had settled into me on a desert highway when I was thirteen years old. My memories of reading the *Diary of a Young Girl* returned as did the promise I had made to Anne to track down a supremeness of being that made room for everyone.

twenty-five

May finally arrived and with it the teaching contract I had worked so hard to acquire. My wide-net search included two independent school job fairs and several in-person interviews from Colorado to Oregon to California. A small school in the Sacramento Valley offered me a position. Trish and I would be within a half-day's drive of many of the destinations we had explored during our first summer together. With Liz and Brad both already settled in the Golden State, I was overjoyed with the outcome.

The long string of goodbyes began at end-of-school functions and family dinners. A Mother's Day's gathering served as the farewell to Ellie, my niece and nephew, and Ellie's three grandchildren. We had one last cookout in the backyard. I had promised to return to Houston every three or four months to spend days with Momma. Was I abandoning her? Yes. I made a choice that was not easy, but Ellie's support of my decision was the green light that allowed me to proceed without regret.

A last supper was necessary with my uncle and aunt who had moved from Chicago to Houston many years ago. Momma made weekly visits to her brother's house which sat halfway between hers and mine. I provided a meal from our favorite barbeque restaurant and delivered it to their door.

I surveyed the scene: three family elders and me. My aunt, half-perched on her chair, tilted toward her husband. He sat immobile and confined to his power wheelchair. Both he and Momma had received the tainted DNA (an abnormality on chromosome 17) from their paternal grandfather, whom they were discussing at the moment and whose eternal salvation was under scrutiny as we licked bbq sauce off our fingers.

The grandfather-in-question had arrived in Chicago from Sweden knowing two English words: *Got work?* He built a thriving laundry business that served the wealthy residents of Michigan Avenue, but he drank too much. In light of that, the Swedish Baptist church to which he belonged struck him from its rolls. The astute business man, albeit frequently inebriated, suffered from a yet-not-named disease that was passed down to Momma and her brother, which had required that Momma take Darvon, then Tramadol, for decades. Had her grandfather's drinking mitigated his chronic pain?

"Do you think he's in heaven?" My aunt tossed out the question as if it had never been asked since the death of the man nearly fifty years before. My uncle continued to chew the slice of brisket his wife had wedged into his mouth, his head dropping his left ear closer to Momma, suggesting his interest in how his sister would answer.

For any given meal, my aunt fastened my uncle's bib, spooned food into his mouth, cleaned out his nostrils with a paper towel, sighed behind his back, hummed a long and unrecognizable tune, held a straw to his lips, wiped his mouth with a wad of napkins, and occasionally, if the moment allowed, swiped a forkful from her plate for herself. My aunt was as close to an angel as I had ever known. For anyone reading who has served as a caregiver of any kind, know you are an angel. Claim it. Now.

I had spent Saturdays for many years tending on Momma: doing her grocery shopping, doing her laundry, changing her bed sheets, completing projects, writing checks for her bills. When she gave up driving and went into a power wheelchair, her reliance on others sky-rocketed. Ellie and I agreed that my move would require a paid caregiver so the burden wouldn't fall to Ellie alone. Momma still put her full reliance in the Lord, and her faith did indeed become her superpower, but Medicaid provided the hands-on caregiving for the time being.

Momma kept mouthing her baked potato, sour cream puddling in the corner of her lips as she considered her sister-in-law's question. She conjured the trance-like stare that she had been able to produce ever since I could remember. When I was a girl, I watched her fixate on a point, usually a knot in the paneling, for minutes at a time. The disembodying effect was scary until I learned to mimic the effort and discovered its mystifying effect.

Momma snapped back. She must have reached a conclusion. Wiping her mouth on the edge of her bib, she proclaimed, "I believe he is. He *is* in heaven." She dug into the cole slaw, spooning a haystacked heap into her mouth. I sat amazed at my mother's certainty, her silent reasoning, her pronouncement that her grandfather would greet them in heaven. Could I coax her to let Anne in, too?

Any sense of nostalgia vanished with the final garage sales, Goodwill drops, curbside freebies, and multiple trips to the dump. Our vision of the future required us to limit our belongings to what could fit in a modest moving container and the backs of our two compact vehicles. The container would be held in Houston storage for the eight weeks, allowing for our stint at the cabin before heading farther west to California.

Trish and Mocha would stay behind for a couple days to complete the final checklist, which insured an empty, clean, and welcoming house for its new owner. Alone, I left Houston with my trusty Subaru packed to the gills in the middle of torrential rains that had flooded the landscape. The hugs and blessings from the women friends who were so dear to me cushioned my heart and strengthened my spine for the journey.

My final goodbye was to the neighbors across the street who had become faithful friends and whose children had grown up alongside mine. The family had been by my side through the passage of time and many ordeals. Our children had grown up together, and their presence had given me a sense of safety and stability that only good neighbors can. Most importantly, they accepted my life with Trish, no questions asked. Any future trip to Houston would not be complete without a cup of coffee at their kitchen table or a libation in the tropical paradise of their backyard.

Highway 287 heading northwest was a parking lot the day I left Houston. I had traveled this trek dozens of times with Trish over the years, always thankful when the road narrowed and the traffic thinned. Certain rest stops and road signs offered the consolation of the familiar. I never tired of grinning at the Cowboy Churches with their dark metal silhouettes of a man and horse kneeling at the cross or at the Jolly, Texas, interstate turnoff sign or the outer-spacey nothingness of northeastern New Mexico near the Capulin Volcano.

"This is going to be your last road trip to the cabin from Houston," Trish had reminded me before I pulled out of the driveway. I'd like to say I remember listening to an audio book or my favorite CDs on that solitary drive to Colorado. The truth is that I drove in silence with a sense of overwhelming relief from leaving what was in the rearview. The sky was barely wide enough to hold my gratitude.

Early during our cabin stay, we boarded Mocha in Denver and flew to California for a few days of house-hunting in three-digit heat. We were clueless about the region's blistering summers. The day before we were to depart after having no luck finding a house we could afford and visualize ourselves owning, we walked into a cool, south-facing living room shaded by a front porch a mere mile from where I would work and knew we had found home. A large fenced backyard would give Mocha the freedom we desired for her.

From the cabin that summer, Trish and I navigated the long-distance purchase of our California home. Our closing date would coincide with our cabin departure in August. We sunk into Colorado time for the weeks of July. The land and sky did their best to cure us from the year just past. I reconstituted myself with hiking and writing and art, and Trish sunk into deep afternoon naps and sunset walks with Mocha.

I spent time with Patrice at our annual San Luis Valley Writing Retreat, an event that we conceived for ourselves and as righteous a writing retreat as I have ever experienced. We fancied long stretches of writing time, morning hikes, French linen lunches with healthy fixin's, drumming, archery, collage, creature sightings, card readings, dinner with wine and a toke or two, but mostly the honesty that had grown between us. Laughter, tears, stars, all from the beauty of Graceland, Patrice and husband Bill's acreage on the edge of Mount Blanca.

Patrice and I loved each other like sisters and talked about our own sisters, how we wished we were closer to them. We agreed that you can't have too many sisters, those intrepid beings who keep believing in who you are. I thanked God in all Her mighty glory for arranging my introduction to Patrice and my other courageous, intuitive friends. We said YES and a friendship began. I thought about how I had found friends like Anne in Patrice, my Washington crew, and my Houston peeps. We had all arrived in each other's lives with full hearts and waiting ears, believing in the power of the inalienable right to share our truths with love and humor.

The big departure day from Circle Dance Ranch arrived with the perennial good weather of August. California waited four state lines away. Trish and I gassed up our two-car caravan for the drive west over multiple passes. Mocha rode with Trish, and I had hours and hours to let my mind run free.

twenty-six

From Daddy, I had learned the love of being behind the wheel. From Sunday drives out to the Hill Country from San Antonio to our frequent trips to Memphis from northern Mississippi to our journeys back to the Midwest to our bicoastal camping adventures, Daddy stayed poised and attentive in the driver's seat. I had learned to do the same. I frequently checked the side mirrors and the rearview, watched the horizon for a weather report, and gave the semis wide berth whenever they drew near. The hum of the pavement offered a meditative backdrop to long drives, and when silence overtook the car's interior, I melded to the landscape like an ant, letting the accelerator do its work, and put my senses on hold. All that remained were faint questions circling like hor d'oeuvres on the lazy susan of my mind.

What makes the heart know where home is? What outlives the goodbyes, the emptying of closets, the guns hung in parallels above the sofa, the spinning wheel, the grandfather's Bible on proud display? Does every home have its middle of the night fears, its dropped breadcrumbs, its bollweevils? Does every home have its dying vines, its collection of keys that no one will claim? its damaged circuits? its wish to be known? its fate to be forgotten?

I wondered many things across the vastness that leads toward the Pacific and barreled into the folds in my memory, the bank in my brain, back to those old roads that I knew by heart, streets making a case for home, what it isn't and what it can be.

I had learned that so many lives had been shoved into train cars, marched over miles, or tossed on the seas. From the Holocaust to the Indian Removal Act to the Atlantic slave trade, recent history had plenty of reminders of how many woundings still coursed through human veins from betrayals and violence done to people not unlike you and me.

The forced removals that invaded so many family stories was a powerful flashpoint of connection among immigrants, refugees, and conscientious objectors of many stripes and from many generations. Beyond religion, nationalism, geopolitics, and economics, those who have been disenfranchised share the grief of being torn from home. I had learned that my story and Anne's story crossed paths in that intersection of loss, of having to say goodbye to what is known and hello to what is not.

Here I was, rolling toward California with my beloved and our dog following in my tracks. I had rejected my claim to anything I had previously known as home. Minnesota, Mississippi, and Texas were now in the rearview. Cemeteries in Illinois, Minnesota, and Wisconsin held the bones of my foremothers, their stories submerged in the deep water of my family's past. Those brave women had made urgent exits from Sweden and Norway with no guarantees. Two of my great-grandmothers died in their thirties far from their Scandanavian homelands, fatalities of the American dream. I was the offspring of leavers, desperate ones who risked failure, who rerouted the family story toward new plots and new languages and new loves.

With the desert conquered, the Eastern Sierra range rose to meet us, and Interstate 80 transformed into miles of curves and rises blasted from mountainsides. Windows down for a whiff of the evergreens and a taste of the chilly air, I turned on the CD player. An Iris Dement ballad blared: "Sing the Delta." A new river delta awaited me, but the delta of my youth was lodged in my soul. When the song ended, I paused in prayer. *Thank you, Infinite Spirit, for getting me here in one piece.* My religious roots had taught me above all else to be grateful. And I was. By nightfall, we had crossed into Sacramento County. I wondered what it would be like to call this new landing place home.

∞

twenty-seven

Life in Sacramento Valley ushered us into the privilege of West Coast living. The beauty of the region, rich as it was, left little trace of its original human inhabitants and their centuries' long imprint on the natural habitats of the region. According to the State of California Native American Heritage Commision, the Nisenan, Me-wuk, Washoe, and Maidu have lived sustainably in the area for over two-thousand years. From the early part of the nineteenth century onward, intruders disrupted their communities and caused a rash of indefensible transformations of their home ground. Tragically, in 1833, not long after the first invaders arrived on the scene, an epidemic of either smallpox or fever killed about 20,000 of the local indigenous inhabitants. The surviving native population was helpless against future expansion. Explorers, fur trappers, cattle ranchers, miners, entrepreneurs, developers, and financiers altered the landscape to mirror their definitions of progress. The First Peoples had not heard of Manifest Destiny yet their story was to be shaped by it.

Thanks to Native Land Digital's resources,[50] I discovered I had lived on lands overtaken from the Wahpekute (Minneapolis), the Choctaw, the Chickasaw (Jackson, Clarksdale, Oxford), the Coahuiltecan, the Caddo (Houston, San Antonio, Tyler) the Jacarilla Apache, the Ute (rural southern Colorado). My displacements had been minor considering the upheavals these groups had suffered. I hoped to be a mindful caretaker of our small lot of soil in deference to the idea that land is not to be possessed but shared.

Even though California entered the Union as a free state, a look at the state's history of political party strength revealed a divide that stretched from its founding to this very day. My assumption that I was entering a

---

[50] Native Land Digital is a Canadian not-for-profit organization that is Indigenous-led. Learn more at native-land.ca

progressive zone was apparently wrong.

Our new neighborhood had initially been a white-flight bedroom community with original covenants in the property records to prove it.[51] Despite the subsequent amendments, the origins were clear. A good number of the original owners were still in the neighborhood. Families of color rarely appeared except to venture in daylight down our street from a cluster of apartments to the nearby park and elementary school. No doubt we were the only same-sex couple for blocks. As much as I loved the cottage we found, I blamed myself for steering us here. Our primary house-hunting search filter was for a home close to the school where I would be teaching. I was an easy mile from work, and soon I would see that our neighborhood and my new school were closer than I thought.

My job, the entry point for our ability to purchase a home and settle ourselves as Californians, placed me in the role of a sixth-grade homeroom teacher in a k-8 religious school at a significant reduction from the salary I had earned in Houston. I hadn't expected to adjust my income so severely, but I trusted the process, even though the numbers didn't lie and neither did the cost of living.

I focused on the agreeable aspects of the situation: joining a less affluent school culture, which suggested to me a significant easing of stress. Prestige no longer appealed to me as a professional perk.

I assumed that the new school, which did not sit at a major intersection of an old money neighborhood like my Houston job had, would be California casual. I was mistaken. Before long, the challenges of my new position outpaced any I had experienced in my lengthy teaching career.

I had to keep more of myself to myself, an expectation that wearied me most. "We don't talk about our personal lives around here," the principal had explained as she tapped her pencil when I urged her to weigh in on my same-sex relationship status during my job interview. I should have heard the warning siren, but at the time, I was tone deaf to anything but a contract offer.

After having a couple weeks to unpack the moving container and get

---

[51] Racially restrictive covenants, which were part of a racist system called redlining, were used in the first half of the 20th century as a way to keep non-White groups out of certain neighborhoods.

a semblance of order in our new house, I prepared myself to buck up for the school year. At the first teacher meeting, I saw that the dress code was not as I had assumed. The uniformly lithe faculty modeled pricey linens and toeless heels, their hair colors sporting shades of fawn and flax, their skin tinted with beachy tans. I quickly scheduled salon appointments for a mani-pedi and highlights and restocked my mascara and lipstick. I didn't want to draw attention to myself. Thank goodness I had packed along a couple weeks worth of trendy warm weather wear from Houston. Lighter hair, tinted nails, heeled sandals, flouncy skirts and loose jackets would have to do until I got a better sense of the look required of me. How does a full-figured, nearly 6-foot-tall woman with a Southern accent slip under the radar? And why was I, at fifty-seven years old, so worried about fitting in?

I had to do what I could to mitigate judgment. New teachers were often targets for vocal, opinionated students, parents, and colleagues. Social media multiplied the threat. The best I could do was keep my nose clean and show up on time with a smile on my face, which was exactly what I intended to do. I couldn't be distracted by mind games.

Within a couple weeks of the start of school, my schedule became routine After a 4 A.M. wake up to write my script for the day, a walk with Mocha at first morning light, and abbreviated morning coffee with Trish, I tightened the straps on a pair of sassy size 10 sandals, blotted a swipe of coral lipstick, and grabbed a chocolate protein drink from the fridge, shaking it with one hand as I pushed open the backdoor with the other. "Off to the races!" I hollered, adding a peppy "I'll be back, y'all!" as a prayer. *You can do this,* I whispered as I loaded my book bag into the back seat. I had never thought of myself as a cheerleader, but what teacher isn't?

I shifted into reverse as the dashboard clock clicked to 7 A.M., then headed into the sun. I endured a long line of firsts in the opening month of the school calendar, and today would add the umpteenth Holy Eucharist.

I hadn't been prepared for the ritualistic propensities of the religious school community I had joined. After years of grappling with the incongruence between my own religious upbringing and my interest in rational thinking, I thought I had already maneuvered the uneven terrain between faith and reason. All ways are good, I had concluded long ago. But I knew I could never return to a faith that repressed the authority of women and stifled their selfhood. I had grown weary of hymns populated with fathers and sons and brothers, the Hims and Hes of salvation. How different the world might be if girls could see themselves in the Trinity.

"I forgot what I'm supposed to do if I don't want to take communion," a new sixth grader, a spindly Jewish girl, confessed to her pony-tailed, cross-necklaced classmate as my homeroom moseyed toward the church to keep our regular chapel appointment. I shortened my stride to match the girls' pace and perked up my ears as we walked through the courtyard approaching the "no talk" zone that was monitored by the school commandant, a retired, buzz-cutted Air Force officer who now enforced traffic and fire drill rules in this conservative kingdom.

"Just cross your arms like this." The answer came with flamboyant choreography and the confident swing of her ponytail. The frozen position mimicked the act of protection I had myself practiced in front of the bathroom mirror not more than an hour before, after an internet search.

I edged in on the conversation. "Do you feel comfortable with that, Rachel?" I asked as I gently touched her shoulder. She nodded and the two separated and scurried ahead on their tiptoes.

I was still learning the rote required in the liturgical version of worship, an elaborate script of declarations more highfalutin' than the "Amen, Brother" gospel services of my youth. This would be my first communion day in a very long time, one that promised to put me and everyone else in the spotlight for a few seconds.

Every student and teacher was required to walk the center aisle to receive the sacraments from the chaplain, who was also the school's Bible teacher. She moved like a white-tented mountain, a half-speed meanderer who intentionally paused between words. Rumor had it that she would be married soon, but that information was only whispered in limited company in the teacher workroom. The school would not publicize a wedding between women.

After the sermon and congregational readings from the Book of Common Prayer, piano strains began. With the fifth graders already rising to move toward the communion table, I waited for the intuitive nudge to stand, signaling to my class that they should rise, too. We filed in a line, the class in front of me, a bobbing single-file of red sweatshirts completed with khaki skirts or pants, cementing the divide. No gender spectrum here. I towered behind the class wearing a dark skirt, pullover sweater, and floral scarf, the swish of my tights rubbing against my thighs with every step I took.

Ahead, the students were on their best behavior, knowing that all eyes in the sanctuary were on them. For the kindergarteners in the front row to the parents in the back to all the students in between, the entertainment of the moment was to watch the exchange of want for wafer and for what would happen next. As the line dwindled in front of me, I stepped closer and closer to the encounter I had been dreading for days.

I crossed my arms, flattening my hands against opposite shoulders as I faced the school chaplain's grey eyes and translucent skin. She offered the promised blessing, one that I expected to make me wince. It didn't. As I turned, my arms fell, and I walked as softly as I could with my eyes following the dark carpet of the side aisle. As I entered the pew, the Jewish girl caught my eye, we shared mock smiles, and I realized how much she looked like photographs I had seen of Anne.

During ongoing monthly communion chapels, I continued to cross my arms against the wafer while colleagues made dramatic signs of the cross and teethed their crackers on the return to their seats. An undercurrent of separateness dug into me. We were from different clans. I knew it, and they did, too.

As my first year at the religious school unfolded, I remained true to my conviction to refuse the sacraments. I had conquered the hold of external expectations. Or so I thought. By March, my dread of communion had become a middle school bully that bore down on me, pelting me, taunting me for my defiance. "Take this my body, given for you!" the monster howled.

Here I was in California, a grown woman with plenty of miles behind her. My history with the Christian faith had ended with its rejection of whom and how I loved. If I were ever to reconcile, it would require the open arms of Jesus welcoming me "just as I am." That hadn't happened yet. Still, I was stressed with how much of an oddball I was at work. I needed to lighten my emotional load and fast.

Fatigued by the growing teacher expectations as the year's end drew near, I rationalized that taking communion could go far in knocking the boulder of nonconformity off my back. My constitution was failing.

After months of crossing my arms against the grain, I rationalized that I would surrender to the ritual in honor of my grandfather, who had died during the Lenten season the month before I was born. "Brother Bill" had been a ghostly character in my life. Momma displayed her father's Bible and portrait prominently in an arrangement she recreated in every one of our many homes. Momma gave me the middle name Hope in the throes of her grief. I was delivered on a river of tears and tagged with an ever-present reminder of the death of the great man of faith whom Momma adored. My name required much of me. Sharon Hope carried a heavy load.

On the communion closest to Easter, I dressed in a white button-down shirt and black skirt, sporting fresh highlights and an extra bit of lipstick. I tried to banish thoughts of Rachel, the Jewish girl, who over the months had grown an even more striking resemblance to Anne Frank.

The chaplain reared backward in surprise when I extended my cupped hands for her favor. After a nod and smile, she pressed the wafer into my palm. Did she suspect that I had succumbed to peer pressure or was she imagining conspicuous repentance, a prodigal daughter? Little did she know I was acting out of self-preservation.

A couple seventh-grade girls jabbed each other as I entered the sixth-grade pew in front of them. *Did you see?* their eyes seemed to signal. *She took the wafer! She took it! She's one of us now.* I dared not make eye contact with Rachel.

Once back in the sixth-grade row, a chill spread into my shoulders as I bowed my head low to stretch my taut muscles. I told myself that the act of contrition didn't mean anything. Anyone in her right mind might do the same under the circumstances. Some might call it acquiescence. Others might call it weakness. I called it a bloodthirsty taste for survival.

twenty-eight

The demands of my first teaching year bled into the next, and my resolve to live under the radar and be a compliant vassal was under threat. On weekday mornings, I addressed myself in the bathroom mirror after brushing my teeth. *You are a superstar, that's what you are!* I chanted.

I chaperoned the January sixth-grade trip to an outdoor education site in the Santa Cruz mountains, an experience I had enjoyed the year before. This year, overlapping demands and deadlines wouldn't let me catch my breath. Calendar tasks required me to carry my retreat gear in one hand and my school bag in the other. Completed grade reports with personalized narrative comments required for more than eighty students across three grade levels would be due upon my return. My bunk turned into a desk at dawn and after lights out. I had fallen victim to my own expectations and couldn't jump off the Type-A train no matter how I tried.

A week later, after my grades and comments were approved, I sought the support of my peers. I wanted to share my story, to be heard, so I invited the sixth-grade teachers to lunch in my classroom. Could we reflect on this stretch of the year, which was for me a month-long nightmare? Word got out that I had, in the words of the administration, "scheduled a teacher meeting without permission."

On a dreary February day between cafeteria duty and my next class, the Assistant Head called for me. Rain pelted my umbrella on my way from the classroom building to the office, the passageway offered no awning, no shelter from the storm. I sat with my hands in my lap as the pert and pretty Assistant Head's brown eyes ground me down to the size of an acorn. I was upsetting the apple cart. Why would I do such a thing?

I told her my story of overwhelm, as I had with my colleagues, then uncrossed my legs, hooked my hands over my kneecaps, and leaned forward.

"There is something else." My eyes caught a sunny spot on the carpet as I confessed. "I'm dealing with a family issue right now. My father's just been diagnosed with cognitive decline." There. That should do it, I thought.

The designated disciplinarian leaned forward and pressed her manicured hand onto mine. "You must be under a lot of stress over that."

"You can't imagine." I stretched upward out of the chair, preparing to exit. "As my sister puts it, we have to get to know our new Dad." I smoothed my skirt and cast my eyes beyond her to the open door.

The Assistant Head was quick on her feet. "I can understand why you might feel frustrated."

I nodded compliantly and said one last thing, "I acted out of turn. It won't happen again." A nod and a gentler gaze saw me out.

I left the administrative suite and immediately went into the bathroom across the hall to wash my hands good and long with hot water and a double dose of soap. I had never been tagged as a rabble-rouser and was still in shock that I had been called in for a dressing down about a lunch invitation to peers.

A line had been drawn in the mud between the front office and me. As I walked back to the classroom that I shared with four other teachers, I hoped I would have a moment to brush the bother off my shoulder. Since succumbing to the communion ritual nearly a year before, I had compromised the self-imposed rules that had gotten me through my job search in the first place: be honest and be yourself. Why hadn't I defended my reality? Why had I invoked Daddy's illness to upload sympathy? How much self-forgetting would I allow?

I mulled those questions for weeks and avoided conversations with colleagues who knew of the rumored insurrection. The ground under my feet shifted and a sense of alienation grew like a boil in my belly. I concentrated my energies on orchestrating the extensive Civil Rights unit. Grammar classes proceeded into the complexities of clauses, and language arts barreled through a journalism unit that had students investigating youthful social change agents like Malala Yousafzai and Iqbal Masih.[52] The content of my

---

[52] Malala Yousafzai, the youngest Nobel Prize laureate, is a Pakistani activist for female education. Iqbal Masih, a Pakistani Christian boy who became a symbol of abusive child labor in Pakistan, was assassinated at the age of twelve for his activism.

classes energized me, but collegiality had all but disappeared. Even those who commiserated with me only extended understanding at happy hours a safe distance from the school. I had promised myself that I would stick it out in this position for two years and then reassess. By February, four months before the two-year mark, my reconsideration accelerated.

The pressures of school multiplied during the Lenten season, and my anxiety had rocketed since the *talking to*. Had Daddy ever felt this kind of frustration? I wondered. How good it would have been to be able to ask for his advice. What did he do when he felt hemmed in? We didn't have such conversations, so the aggravations of his career would be lost on me. I had to rely on myself.

Ellie and I consulted about how to best manage our new list of obligations in Minnesota. We made separate visits to St. Paul in the winter to form a baseline plan with the help of Nina, Jane's daughter. How could we support Daddy and Jane in their transition to a smaller home and make sure Daddy had the medical support he needed? We would make a joint visit to St. Paul in June since Jane was chomping at the bit to sell the house and get Daddy's condition managed. The biggest complication would be Daddy. He didn't want to move and had refuted the idea like I had refuted his transfer from Clarksdale to Oxford. I understood. Daddy didn't want to leave home.

twenty-nine

April appeared with its promises of California poppies in the garden and strawberries in the colander, a month of blossoms and blessings, of sun and saviors, reviving eyes and ears and appetites. The mockingbird sang under the light of the moon. All manner of green, tender and bright, flooded the landscape while honey-baked hams, shortcakes, and whipping cream found themselves in shopping carts all over town. Easter beckoned, but my hope for resurrection was dull.

My body, mind, and spirit slumped into the sofa, my book bag weighting my lap as the weekend began. Good Friday was anything but, and the calendar taunted me with two more months before summer vacation. Beyond all the grading was a class anthology to format, proofread, and publish, and four final exams to write, complete with study guides. Burnout pursued me like a rabid wolf, but I was too tired to notice.

When her doctor confirmed that Trish's stem cell transplant recovery was complete, she secured a school counselor position at the best secular independent school in town and was thriving during our second year in California. Her spring break didn't coincide with mine, so she made plans to travel. In late March, Trish traveled east with Mocha across the mountain passes to the cabin to complete a couple indoor projects and see Colorado friends during what was still winter there. I had the house to myself for a full ten days. The spaciousness and shift in routine ramped up my skills of introspection.

In Trish's absence, I searched my heart for alternatives to the cage that trapped me. How long could I tolerate the status quo? Holy Week approached as I grappled with the Future Tense of My Life. What I wanted was rest. I had been on Transition Road for three years now, unsettled and shuffling my actions to meet The Next Big Thing.

On Good Friday, the day before Trish would arrive home from her trip, the sound of an early morning garbage truck jarred me from a dream. *An ocean rises into my workspace. I meet with others who seem oblivious to the flood even as things are being lifted off the floor by the water, which flows in from an endless sea. The unstoppable waves push me toward safety, toward anchor. Don't fight—float, the waves advise.*

On Holy Saturday, Trish texted that she had crossed back into California. In the early afternoon, she began to send regular updates: *darn traffic at a stand still...big fender bender....all three lanes at a dead stop, dang it, dang it, dang it...eighty-six miles to go... would you rather be at home or stuck in this madness?*

To that I texted back: *I'm happy right where I am. Would you rather have a girlfriend who is employed or one who is living off her retirement in search of her future?*

Her reply: *I always believe in the search, wherever it leads.*

On Easter, I spent the morning writing my resignation letter with the plan that I would deliver it the next day. Trish applauded the final result. The letter ended with a statement as honest as I had ever made, "I will depart with a sense of sadness, but am certain that my choice will be one that I will never regret." My letter was accepted with little fanfare and a few kind hugs. Somehow I survived the final push toward the end of school: another outdoor education trip, open house, 8th grade graduation, a public farewell, and the last bloody communion of my life.

The June heat kicked up from the driveway as I unpacked my book collection and desk organizer from the car. I remembered that Trish would not be home until later, that I would need to walk Mocha. What better way to celebrate my last official day of teaching than a walk with the precious creature who'd been with me through it all: Trish's chemo and transplant, the farewell to Houston, cabin summers, the first two years in California, and now, the halt of my teaching career. Mocha had been and would continue to be a guide and teacher for me. Her tail wagged expectantly as I put on my walking sandals and hat and grabbed my car keys so we could enjoy the cool of the river.

Mocha and I found our favorite trail. We climbed the slight rise where the almond trees had blossomed weeks ago and where the grasses leveled their slim emerald spikes toward the sun, some standing a foot tall. Two women in burkas collected wildflowers in a field near the parking lot while a young college-aged Black couple wearing explosive smiles carried beach bags toward the sandbar. Mocha pulled toward the pond and the honks of Canada geese. The cloudless sky hovered above choppy water as a great egret lifted from near the shore. Summer!

I didn't know what life would look like in two months when I wouldn't be getting a planner in order or looking over my class lists to highlight which of my students had parents on the Board. The sense of relief rubbed into my shoulders like a good massage. I wanted to get a tattoo, let my hair go white, and have a shock of blue alter my profile. And what I wanted I just might get.

We heard the river before it came into view, snowmelt bursting against the boulders, the rapids joyful. All I knew as Mocha and I stepped into an eddy near the shore was that I wanted to take a slow boat into my future this time around and let decisions melt like butterscotch in my mouth before I swallowed.

One thing Trish and I had decided after I submitted my letter of resignation was that our budget would require a short-term infusion to cover costs during what I termed my intermission. I already had June, September, and October trips to St. Paul on my schedule with trips to see Momma in Houston sandwiched between. How would I possibly manage a new job in light of all that? I decided I wouldn't.

Trish admitted, after returning from her cabin trip, that the drive was much longer and more demanding than driving to Colorado from Houston had been. Then, she enumerated the cabin repairs we were going to need in the next few years, several including substantial investment.

"What if we sold the place and split the proceeds three ways, a third for the household, a third for me, and a third for you?" she asked me one morning during our coffee time.

I was stunned. "Give up the land? For what!" I squealed. Mocha yelped at the snap in the air.

"Freedom!" she added another high pitch to the scene. "How good would it feel not to worry about your bills and have a cushion to cover all your travel?" Clearly she had been thinking about this for a while.

"That's a lot to consider," I had to admit. My coffee had cooled so I took a long sip. We explored the idea. Could we really give up what we had made together up in those Colorado foothills? How could we abandon the sublime monotony of it? Was I willing to exchange privilege for solvency? The answer was yes. We had invested money and time into Circle Dance Ranch, and we knew we could get a good return on the investment. We weren't getting any younger, and it was time for us to pare down our footprint on the planet.

Over dinner a few days later, we toasted the cabin, the trailer, our precious eleven acres, and our decision to sell. After some personal time I had scheduled for myself, and my upcoming June trip to St. Paul, we would spend our last summer at Circle Dance Ranch, preparing for new owners, whom we hoped would love it like we did.

thirty

To commemorate my separation from teaching, I scheduled a three-day silent retreat for myself at a rural hermitage in the Santa Lucia Mountains near Big Sur. New Camaldoli offered sleeping rooms with individual private gardens overlooking the Pacific. To get there, I would be required to take a circuitous route since the coastal highway had been closed both north and south by landslides. The registrar apologized for the travel complications and offered to change my reservation dates because of the treacherous nature of the only mountain road that connected the valley with Big Sur. Nothing was going to deter me from the personal time that I needed. I could handle it, I assured her.

Trish took my car in for a tune-up and reminded me of her mantra, "Safety first!" as I pulled out of the drive that Sunday morning.

When I was seventeen, Daddy taught me how to operate a standard shift subcompact, a welcome replacement for the Plymouth Belvedere that drew wolf whistles from truckers but jeers from my peers.

When Daddy folded himself into the passenger seat of the tiny Toyota sedan for my manual shift lessons, his knees nearly met his chin. He had to hang his right arm out of the passenger-side window to have the wiggle room he needed to instruct me. The fits and starts of my first moves with a clutch must have knocked him silly, but he never let on. Daddy was a good teacher, patient and technically focused. I felt pride in knowing how to shift gears, something many people my age never learned to do.

The two-hundred-mile journey to New Camaldoli was slowed by back ups, crashes, and roadside fires. My ability to translate details into metaphor put me on high alert. I arrived at the crossroad I needed to drive west and downshifted as I mouthed its name. Na-ci-mi-en-to. Na-ci-mi-en-to. Five syllables and eighteen treacherous miles between me and the sea.

The sun angled its trickster shadows through the dense forest and onto the narrow asphalt as my aging Subaru climbed in second gear, switchback after switchback. I shifted into third for the longer stretches. My nerves tangled with each approaching vehicle, most populated by wild hearts rushing with youthful abandon away from the dipping sun that I was creeping toward.

Something told me I would feel better with the windows down. I was right. The smell of the coastal forest revived me. My shades came off, and I accelerated. No more fighting the strobing sun. I focused on the dips and curves and not on the cliff sides and slide warnings. So little lay between my moving hunk of metal and the Great Beyond. I concentrated on what I could see.

Once the wooded hills gave way to a bluing horizon, I thought I just might make it if I held onto the steering wheel and stayed in low gear for the final descent. Nacimiento had humbled me. I had crossed the threshold and entered my retreat on that old mountain road.

I stood outside Room 9 and pondered its name: Immaculate Heart. Once inside, I smiled at the simple furnishings and the wall of windows that looked out onto the private garden and the Pacific bowl of blue. An image of a gentle Christ, not a crucified one, hung above the twin bed, cradle for my stay. After situating my things, I created an altar. On the desk that faced the window, I placed a woven purple scarf, a quartz rock from Colorado, and a red lantern that had been a gift from Patrice. From my walks, I would later add fresh findings: feather, fern, flower.

In the evening light, I sat in the garden as jays and sparrows flitted in the brush and bees buzzed in blooms. The Pacific rounded the view. I had fallen hard for Big Sur's beauty when I had discovered it decades before.

As newlyweds in our early twenties, my young husband and I had driven thirty-seven hours straight in our wild escape from East Texas to Monterey toward his Naval training at the Defense Language Institute. Our marriage ended after eleven years, but the legacy of our life in California lived on. I would be forever grateful that we had discovered the central Pacific coast when we did and how we did. Ray and I had driven down the coast to Big Sur on many a weekend. We couldn't get enough of the spectacle. Coastal grandeur spread its feast, and we devoured it. The royal meeting of mountain and sea with its incomprehensible horizon offered a spiritual sensuality that fed my kinship with the divine.

Why I was on a silent retreat in the first place had its roots in my ongoing friendship with Patrice. Our lives had continued to intertwine after we each left the high school where we taught. Early in our friendship, we discovered Parker Palmer's *The Courage to Teach* together, longing to more fully incorporate reflection and the courage of conviction into our lives as educators. As a result, Patrice suggested that we journal about our teaching experiences. We did and were inspired! Patrice ended up completing her Master's thesis with the focus of Professional Reflective Journaling. A profound trust developed between us and our collaboration grew into offerings of journaling workshops for teachers, presentations at national conferences, and more importantly, a friendship that held our deepest hopes and fears.

A peripheral effect of facilitating workshops with Patrice was that I learned how to create and nurture sacred space. She insisted on draping our workshop meeting tables with colorful scarves, adding centerpieces of wildflowers and candles, ringing chimes, and scattering quotes by Pema Chodron, Paolo Friere, bell hooks, Audre Lorde, Mary Oliver, Wislawa Szymborska and others whose words expanded possibility and deepened introspection. I absorbed these discoveries like a newborn and began to create and tend altar spaces on my own.

My respect for author and mentor, Parker Palmer, had nudged me to explore an organization he had founded, The Center for Courage and Renewal. I registered for an annual season of four vocational recharge retreats in Washington State, and then another, and another. I became part of a Courage and Renewal circle of trust, that reinforced the importance of aligning my core beliefs with my actions and of doing that in community with like-minded others. Courage work exposed me to other guides and mentors: Wendell Berry, John Lewis, Desmond Tutu, Terry Tempest Williams, Joanna Macy, and more.

I had arrived at a place in time when it made perfect sense to be on spiritual retreat in a place of great beauty to acknowledge in solitude and silence all that had supported my years of teaching. The longing in my soul was eased when I spent time in communion with sacred creation.

As a guide for my retreat, I brought Richard Rohr's companion journal to *Falling Upward: A Spirituality for the Two Halves of Life*. In Rohr's contemplative text were journaling questions, experiential exercises, and quotations to assist readers toward reflection, the reason I was there. I responded to prompts like this one: "The very first sign of the potential hero's journey is that he or she must leave home....Can you identify a wound in your life that has opened you up to a whole new understanding? How has it shaped the person you have become?" I envisioned *The Diary of a Young Girl* in one hand and my worn red leather Bible in the other, not as counterpoints, but rather as parts of a puzzle I had been trying to solve for decades. What was it that Anne had written? *"I don't think of all the misery but of all the beauty that remains."*

My search for a god bigger than any religion had begun with a promise to a Jewish girl from Amsterdam and had grown into a pilgrimage toward all that is holy. "Faith is simply to trust the real, and to trust that God is found within it," Rohr attests. I circled those words, closed my journal and breathed the truth of that as the surf pounded the rocks below.

On the final morning of my retreat at the New Camaldoli Hermitage, I sat in the wooden rocker wearing my oversized flannel shirt with a worn fleece blanket on my lap. Mist and fog obscured the sea's expanse and muffled the horizon. I had not considered exactly what form the ceremony of farewell to my career would take. I sat with my coffee in hand, staring into nothingness. Something would come to me.

Symbolism loomed large as I spotted the bright apple that had inadvertently landed on my altar after my earlier dig into the food bag. My body moved toward the lush fruit with a knife. Before I could even think about what I was doing, I cut the Honeycrisp in half, chopped a number of bite-size pieces, counted out twenty-eight, and placed them in a bowl on the altar. I lit the red lantern from Patrice, bowed to the four directions, and partook of one apple piece at a time for each of the years of my teaching career. With each slow bite and swallow, I stopped to recall faces, places, feelings, year by year. I communed in reverence with past challenges, regrets, and triumphs. After the final bites, the least sweet ones, I put the remaining apple half in the bowl, where it would stay until I left the retreat, a visible reminder of life yet to be lived.

The night before my departure, my anxiety about the return on Nacimiento Road ramped up, and my body trembled under the comforter. I dreamed. *Daddy is trying to program a fire alarm. I stand frozen, wanting to step forward but not able. Helpless, I observe from a distance as he tries to figure out the code, but can't.*

The next morning, I made an early departure to avoid traffic, but Nacimiento wasn't finished with me yet. As I maneuvered one of the hairiest curves, the tire light came on. "Damn it!" I shouted. Off went the cd player. With a full ten miles to go before getting over the mountain and another ten through a military installation with no services, I had no other choice but to stop and check the tire pressure every few miles. I hoped for a slow leak and decided to sing. The old favorite taught to me by Grandma Sig rose from my lips with its steadying "whatever will be will be" until a merciful air pump appeared and gave me just enough confidence to keep me driving toward home.

thirty-one

The pact Ellie and I made back in the winter had us convening in St. Paul in late June. Not two minutes after Ellie and I turned into the driveway on Moss Road did we realize our father-daughter reunion had been upended by a power greater than ourselves. Jane. A third of the garage held boxes, furniture, and bulky garbage bags ready for tossing. After hugs and hellos, Jane whispered toward my chin as I steadied her on my arm, "We're cleaning out. The guns have got to go."

Once Ellie and I took in the sights of the spacious backyard, a newly painted deck, the hedge of hostas, the rabbits and squirrels, Ellie's quick mind kicked in, "Daddy, do you think we could take a little drive to the old neighborhood? It's tradition!" Jane wasn't interested in visitations to our past, so the tour would give us time with Daddy alone.

"Well, sure." Daddy answered. "Now?"

Daddy bade Jane farewell, opened the garage door, and before we knew it, our 84-year old father was behind the wheel like old times. He had begun treating himself to late model cars since his marriage to Jane. He was an admitted car fiend and measured his life by cars not years. Daddy showed us the bells and whistles on his latest model. Then, he headed toward Minneapolis. Soon we were parked on Grandma Sig's street. Ellie and I both noted that he hadn't missed a turn.

We stood on the sidewalk arm in arm in front of Daddy's childhood home on a street carved out of the flats south of downtown in the early 1900s. As we took the requisite pictures in front of the bungalow now painted Swedish red, memories rose from the rafters. Peering at the upper floor window, I imagined the room where Ellie slept when we visited as children.

The dormered room, with one small window facing the street, had once displayed on all of its walls our long-dead grandfather's gun collection:

shotguns, rifles, and pistols from the Civil War, the Wild West, and the gangster years. It was a strange place for a girl to be and an even stranger place to sleep. I was happy for my sister to have the room with the view. The guns gave me the creeps. Eventually, Grandma removed the weapons from the walls, tore down the nail-studded wallpaper, and painted the room a cheery yellow. The guns were loaded into a trailer and taken into Daddy's custody. He had hauled the collection from Minnesota to Mississippi to Texas and back to Minnesota again, rarely speaking of them and instructing us never to do so. The guns, a museum of my grandfather's passion, were a family secret. What would people think of an F.B.I. agent who stored an entire arsenal among his things?

I slept in a space of safer angles, pink and gray art deco wallpaper, closets to be invaded. Discovering Grandma's treasures, we sisters modeled her fur coats and formal dresses, clomping down the narrow stairs in Sig's fashionable heels, egged on by her pronouncements of Miss Minnesota or Miss Mississippi, and if we had wowed her completely, the ultimate: Miss America. The miseducation of her two granddaughters was bolstered by the most well-meaning of women. Grandma was an emblem of independence and ingenuity, and her invocation of beauty pageants was meant to connect and encourage, not to undermine. I knew I was not Miss Anything, not with my chubby middle and my overbite. Grandma wanted me to know that I was beautiful to HER.

Grandma Sig stirred up dramatic flair everywhere—in the kitchen with savory meatballs, on the piano with jaunty showtunes, and at the sewing machine with inventive designs like the groovy patchwork wrap skirt that was the envy of every other seventh-grade girl in my class in 1971. As the mother of an only son, Sig had a ball with her grandgirls. From my view, she had created a rich life for herself. She never spoke of herself as a widow and was way too feisty to be weighed down by that label.

She hadn't wanted to wear the orphan label either. Surely remnants remained of her girlhood trauma, but she unburdened herself somehow of the rock quarry accident that killed her father and the broken heart that took her mother not long after. She learned to find her own way. She and her husband ended up in the Twin Cities sixty miles north of the farm town where they met. In time, Duke joined the police force in Minneapolis where records show that he was an expert marksman, the best of the bunch. Had his shooting talents encouraged his interest in collecting guns?

The couple's bungalow sat six blocks from Minnehaha Creek, which tumbled into the magnetic waterfall surrounded by parkland that provided recreational freedom for their only child, Leo. Minnehaha Park followed the creek that emptied into the Mississippi River, the life blood of economies spread over two-thousand miles. As long as the creek fed the river and the river flowed to the Gulf, I would feel the connection it had to our Northern roots and Southern fate.

"Shall we head over to the Falls?" I suggested. Daddy jostled his keys, pressed the unlock key, listened for the beep, and made a slow spin looking for his car.

"Only for a few minutes, Sharon. We have to get over to the storage units before it gets too late." Ellie added, keeping our chores front and center.

Daddy tilted over the counter at the glassed-in office of the Public Storage, his once six-foot, six-inch frame now curved into a hollowing chest, his belt buckled in the last hole and still hanging loose. "We need to rent a small unit," he croaked in a voice that wanted to sound authoritative but instead wavered. Daddy smacked his tongue against the roof of his mouth like he was holding a peppermint there. His hands tightened on the edge of the ledge as he pushed himself upright, age spots blotting his quivering arms. He found a place on the opposite edge of the counter to fix his gaze and stood silent as the desk clerk dug into the files.

After Daddy signed the contract, Ellie grabbed the keys and was out the door with a forced ultimatum, "Let's get this show on the road." The unit secured, we headed back to Moss Road where we were to stow away the forty-something vintage rifles and shotguns that had been crowding a room in the basement before Jane blew a gasket.

First we hauled the guns up from the basement into the garage. Ellie and I avoided eye contact as we squeezed past each other on the narrow basement stairs, empty-handed on the way down and lugging shotguns, long-barrels, heavy with metal and wood, on the way up. I sunk evermore inward with every weapon that passed into my arms. Had Daddy been dragging around a financial investment all these years or was there more to it than that? He had told Ellie on some distant occasion that these guns were like brothers to him. Had his father's gun room quieted a loneliness in him, the single resident of the second floor? Had he wanted to be as important to his father as the guns had been? As admired?

What had they taught him after all this time? Did he know?

Once the basement had been emptied of all but the pistols, Ellie set up the sawhorses and directed the creation of two stations, one for tagging, photographing, and bubble wrapping and one for camouflaging with the bolts of pink-and-blue-striped flannel Ellie had spotted on deep discount as we shopped for packing supplies. The pattern reminded me of something a mother might use to make playful prison uniform costumes for her fraternal twins on Halloween.

Ellie assigned Daddy and me to Station One. His aimless attention held steady only with reminders. *Ready, Daddy? Hold here. That's good. Now here. Perfect.* We worked in quiet syncopation under Ellie's watchful eye. During the tagging, she scribbled notes in the composition book: double barrel. decorative handle, Harper's Ferry, 1857, and so on.

"What do you know about this one?" she asked as she held a rifle close for Daddy's inspection.

He answered, "Nothing."

With the rising temperature in the garage, we raised the door two feet up from the floor and warned each other to be on the lookout for the footsteps of the letter carrier or curious neighbors. In keeping with the longstanding confidentiality agreement, nobody could know our current business.

Jane poked her head into the garage now and then to check our progress. "My god, you're still working?" she observed. We gleamed with sweat, ignoring her.

By early afternoon, we had a carload's worth in the deep trunk of the Buick LaCrosse. Ellie held the keys to the new storage unit, the third in Daddy's growing collection. We drove in silence, unpacked in silence, maneuvered the quilt-covered, unwieldy flatbed cart in silence, and unloaded in silence, making multiple trips, aware of every ne'er-do-well in sight and doing everything we could to conceal our purpose, a father and his daughters packing heat.

Once the guns were stowed away, we spent a good bit of time down in the basement file room. Ellie and I came across things that astounded us, everything from separate file folders for every car Daddy had ever owned to decades of generic disclosures from investment accounts to stacks of old FBI magazines crowded the shelves. Daddy hovered around us with a divided presence, part doting father and part indignant man-of-the-house. We managed the duplicitous energies and bantered back and forth in fun, trying to keep Daddy from getting too focused on findings that he wanted to examine and save. The time for that was past. I understood Jane's frustration. What had kept him from disposing of all this paper? Then BOOM. I came across a file that simply said in all caps: INSTRUCTIONS.

"What's this?" I asked Daddy, holding the manila folder out to him.

He and Ellie circled around, and he took his place between us. He opened the folder to find a short stack of stapled papers, a couple of pamphlets, and a thin red spiral notebook.

"Well, let's see." He lifted the Last Will and Testament of Leo Fabriz. At that, Ellie began to cry. Daddy wrapped his arms around her, and she crumpled into him as I stood there, a motionless bystander to her tears.

Whenever we drove away from Grandma Sig's after our summer visits, Ellie would wail for at least an hour and then relent to sleep. Unlike hers, my feelings were subterranean. Like a desert mammal, I burrowed for water that never made it to the surface and left hollows behind in the process. I wondered if I had left my ability to cry on the horizon of the Mojave the summer of my thirteenth year, when the rules of my religion broke my heart.

"We'll keep this right here," Daddy said, slipping the folder into the small metal file box marked *Things to Keep*.

We left Daddy with a passel of appointments already on the calendar for fall. He and Jane would continue to downsize. Jane's daughter, Nina, would see to it that they toured a few senior apartments in the interim, and we'd be back for the final push. As I boarded my plane, I wondered at what we had accomplished. Daddy was not happy with the idea of moving out of the house and even less happy with having to accept help to do it. I hoped he'd remember that we'd been there, what we'd done with the guns, and that we'd be back again soon.

The cabin sale had been almost immediate. Trish and I convinced the buyer to delay the closing date so that we could stay on the land for a full month to get a semblance of the summer to which we had become accustomed. Thankfully he agreed.

When I returned to Colorado, Patrice and I attended a School of Lost Borders[53] wilderness program on The Art of Storytelling and Listening, a formidable substitute for our annual writing retreat. For the remainder of the summer, Trish and I tried to maintain a healthy balance between the self-indulgence of basking in the final days at Circle Dance and completing the heart-yanking chores required to leave it for good.

---

[53] The School of Lost Borders offers vision fasts and wilderness experiences, which cultivate self-trust, responsibility, and understanding about one's unique place within society and the natural world.

thirty-two

Trish and I savored the road trip back home, taking Mocha to dog parks along the way and making vista stops to stretch for deep breaths. Trish would get back to work, and for the first time in twenty-nine years, I would not. For me, the return to California meant a turnaround back to St. Paul not long after Labor Day for the first in the fall ration of visits that Ellie and I had arranged. She and all of Houston were in massive clean-up and community support mode from Hurricane Harvey[54] and historical flooding, so I would make the next trip alone.

I recalled how certain I had been about quitting my job and couldn't imagine preparing for school on top of tending to the obligations in St. Paul. The easing of stress had already lightened my migraines, those demons that had been stealing two or three days a month from me for years. I boarded the plane without a duffel of student papers to be graded, without lessons to plan. That alone felt like a monumental shift in my air space.

I arrived on Moss Road with much business to complete. I kept lengthy notes so that Ellie and I could keep track of what had been accomplished and what hadn't. A shorthand about Daddy's business went something like this: *13-pound weight loss since June - why?, neurology appt. next month, follow-up pcp in November, Advanced Directive signed and distributed. Daughters added as emergency contacts. Two visits to senior apartment complexes. Daddy's not thrilled.*

After Daddy and I arrived home from the doctor, I asked Jane, behind Daddy's back, to inquire about the appointment so I could hear what he had to say. As we watched through the window the children walking past on their way home from school, Jane cleared her throat to get our attention.

"LEO! What. Did. The. Doctor. Say." She seemed to have practiced. Her

---

[54] Hurricane Harvey was a devastating Category 4 hurricane that made landfall on Texas and Louisiana in August 2017, causing catastrophic flooding and many deaths.

words kept beat with her shaking leg.

I looked at Daddy. He looked at his watch. "What's that?" he said, adjusting his hearing aid and looking up at Jane.

"What. Did. The. Doctor. Say." This time she glared right at me as she spoke. *Do you get it, yet?* her eyes pleaded.

"Oh," he said. "Everything's fine." He put his hands on his knees and stretched into a more prideful pose.

"Daddy?" I held up my notebook. "I took a few notes. I'm going to read them for Jane."

"Oh. Okay." He seemed interested.

That's a good sign, I thought as I began to recite the list: the weight loss, the need for more exercise, the option for using the VA's Memory Clinic, the upcoming neurology appointment.

"Oh, really?" he replied with the delivery of each detail, pursing his lips, narrowing his eyes, rubbing his hands together just like I did when I was nervous.

"You. Know. Sharon." Jane piped up. Her words started flowing. "I saw Ace a few weeks ago. You know who Ace is. He's my lawyer. And I asked him what he thought about a divorce. That's right. A divorce. I can't do this anymore."

Now, I was the one without words. "Oh." I peeped.

Daddy sent his gaze toward the front window and to the neighborhood children's game of chase across the street. Had he heard her or turned his hearing aid off already? I spotted his thumb rubbing his forefinger and guessed. I had that habit, too, when I worried.

"Ace didn't think it was a good idea at my age. But I don't know about that." She shifted in her seat and glared at her husband.

I remembered back to when Ellie and I had visited in June. We convinced Daddy to show us the contents of the original two storage units he had maintained for nearly twenty years, since his mother moved from her house to an apartment. Inside the biggest, a temperature-controlled unit, were the contents, furniture and all, of Grandma's living room. I had asked Daddy if he would consider donating the living room sofa to a shelter to create some walking space. He answered, "I might have to come live here, so no." How could an intelligent, sensible man like Daddy think such a thing?

∞

thirty-three

Ellie and I had separate visits scheduled in November for Daddy's follow-up appointments and finalizing a location for Daddy and Jane's new home. But Daddy's 85th birthday weekend in October felt like a no-brainer. We had to be there together for a happier occasion than the June visit had been, with its heavy artillery of memories.

We arrived to the first snow of the season, the skrim of white foretelling the frozen ground that would follow in the weeks to come. The streets were slippery until the sun won out and dried up the evidence of inevitable winter.

"What about a family history tour?" I propositioned during Sunday brunch at Whole Earth, a second home for Daddy and Jane, who ate out at least once daily. Ellie picked up on the hint and asked Daddy if she could chauffeur us in the rental. Jane opted out, as we had suspected, and we made a quick plan. We would start at the cemetery and end up at the Falls.

The National Cemetery sat adjacent to the airport and not too far from the viewing area where Daddy and his father went to watch the planes in the '40s when Daddy was a boy. Grandma Sig and Grandpa Duke were buried in a section within view of one of the terminals. We read the engravings on the headstones as we had many times before. None of us was going to say it, but we knew that Daddy would be buried in this cemetery someday, too.

"On to happier things?" I suggested. Ellie jingled the keys, and we walked hand in hand, Daddy in the middle, back to the car. Minnehaha Park was emptied of visitors that Sunday morning. What a treat to have the Falls to ourselves. In an effort to evolve the birthday visit into a real celebration, I hollered, "Daddy!" Pick up some leaves!"

"What?" he had asked, unsure and confused.

"Pick up some leaves, Daddy!" I tried again, kicking the leaves at my feet. He folded his withering frame at the waist and scooped up a handful. I intervened. "An armful, Dad! Lots of them!"

He gave me a questioning look but stretched himself down again, this time with a slight squat, getting his elbows involved. "Now what?" he asked, looking at the leaves in his arms and then toward me.

"Toss them! Like this!" I gathered a collection and scattered them wildly. "Way up high!"

I grabbed my phone, found the video setting, and pointed the camera lens just in time to hear his wary but obedient, "Okay." As the leaves went flying from his arms, his expression brightened and supplied me with a boyish smile that would last me a lifetime.

I was to return to St. Paul two weeks after Daddy's birthday weekend for a few more in the battery of chores still undone. Trish had become accustomed to predawn drives to the airport so that I could catch the earliest non-stop flight. In my absence, she would also adapt her schedule to walk Mocha twice a day and adjust her diet to include some easy fast food favorites. The dinner hour wouldn't be the same for either of us. "I'll be back," I promised as I tugged my carry-on from the backseat onto the pavement in the Departures lane. *Love you*, I mouthed over my shoulder as my feet took me through the automatic door to Check In.

The frigid temperatures had Daddy and me outfitted in deep-winter apparel. He wore a fur trapper hat and gloves that made his hands into giant paws. First stop, the VA, which was decked out for Veteran's Day in even more red, white, and blue than usual. Daddy and I spent the morning following arrows from one department to the next in a building that covers 1.5 million square feet. After our three stops there and the hundreds of steps in between, Daddy agreed that I could treat him to lunch.

We stopped at a hip grill that I had been eyeing for months and were seated near the windows at a bar table for two, the chairs just right for our long legs. Daddy ordered an ornate dish of poutine piled with carnitas and glopped with cheddar and sour cream, the fragrance of Texas bringing a grin to his face. "Oh, george!" Daddy exclaimed when the server set down the platter. He dug right in. We did not say grace.

At the bar behind us sat a young man with a shaved head and a Lovecraft[55] monster displayed in full color on the back of the motorcycle jacket that draped from his chair. As a waiter rushed between our table and the bar, the jacket slipped to the floor. I hadn't noticed, but Daddy did.

Before I knew it, Daddy was patting the tough guy on the left shoulder and bending toward his ear. "Don't want you to be startled. Your jacket's on the floor. I'm going to pick it up." Daddy resecured it to the back of the chair, and the dude grinned and nodded in tacit agreement. This was a natural act for Daddy. He was a nice guy who knew how to be kind to strangers, even unapproachable ones.

Near the end of our meal, Daddy leaned forward. "How's your mother?" he asked.

Startled, I delivered a quick "she's doing well" and took a chance. "Wanna see a photo?" A few days before, her caregiver had texted me a picture of Momma with a fresh hairdo. Daddy cradled my phone, holding it close to his face. On the small screen, he saw a chubby, snowy-haired woman outfitted in white, sitting as tall as she could in her wheelchair, her signature burgundy lipstick framing that dimpled smile. Could he still see the woman he had married at 23, over 60 years ago? Not a word had passed between them since the divorce. He had asked about her over the years, but the silence between them had wounded me, and I wasn't crazy about being the only conduit of communication between my parents. Ellie wouldn't discuss either with the other, as far as I knew. She fiercely defended Daddy's willfulness not to engage. I was more pliable. I knew Daddy was angry with Momma, humiliated by her more likely. But he was also angry with a power much greater than my mother—the power that allowed a thirty-year marriage to dissolve, its illusions of happiness traded for what one member of the union believed she deserved: the right to feel loved. Did he take any of the responsibility for the failed marriage or was Momma solely to blame?

Suddenly, I heard my own voice. "You two haven't spoken for so many

---

[55] Howard Phillips Lovecraft (1890 -1937) was an American writer of weird and horror fiction.

years, Daddy." Something egged me on though I didn't know what or why. "It's been hard." I stumbled and dabbed my napkin on my lips, "What if something happens to me or to Ellie or one of the kids? Would you talk to Momma then? What if I died? Would you come to the funeral?" I let loose a time warp of worries that had badgered me the past thirty years.

Daddy put my phone facedown on the table and moved his fork around on his empty plate. "What makes you think those things?" He reached out for my hand.

"It's normal to have questions, Daddy," I answered, squeezing his hand and looking into his eyes, even though it was hard. "I really want to know."

He cleared his throat as he rubbed his thumb and forefinger in slow motion and answered with watering eyes, "We need to talk about it." But we never did.

We watched for ice patches on the way to the car in the parking garage. Daddy patted my shoulder and drew me closer. "I like this place." He fumbled for his keys and pressed the unlock button to flash the lights so he could find his car. He hadn't forgotten how to cover for his losses.

When we arrived home from our lunch, Daddy left the garage door open, an unlikely choice considering the cold. Next thing I knew, he was checking the gasoline in the lawn mower. "What are you doing, Daddy?" I asked, calmly as I could.

"I need to mow down the hedge. It's going to snow." Thirty feet of hostas formed the eastern border of the backyard. I liked that they, instead of a fence, separated the yards between neighbors. In their center sat the concrete birdbath that had been in Daddy's childhood backyard. He had hauled the heavy ornament to Jane's house when Grandma's house sold. Daddy tended the swath of hostas as the custodian of something precious, and it suggested the gentleness that I had known in him when I was a child.

While Daddy pushed the lawnmower into the driveway, I furiously searched for the Twin Cities weather on my phone. "Daddy, we've already reached the high of 19 degrees with no snow expected for at least two days!" I held the weather graphics toward him and mentioned the details with a little more firmness in my voice than before. "No snow for TWO days, Daddy!"

Daddy ignored me and rolled the mower around the corner. I gave up my attempt at redirection. My father was nothing if not stubborn. "You wouldn't believe what Daddy is doing, Jane! Come look!"

From the kitchen, we watched as he wrangled the mower over the crispy brown stalks, leveling the entire swath with the will of a soldier. Amazed at his spunky moves, I snapped photos from the closest window as I cooked up a story to tell him later.

Once he was back inside and settled in his favorite chair with a soda can beside him, I made an announcement. "I called Channel 11 and told them to send a reporter to Moss Road ASAP!" I had learned from Daddy that embellishment was the hallmark of a good joke. "A news truck is on its way!"

"Oh, really? What's the story?" he asked. Was he playing along or did he really wonder?

"An eighty-five-year-old veteran was seen mowing down hosta stalks in 19 degrees!" I reported.

He grinned. I insisted I was serious. He examined my face for so long that I couldn't help but break into laughter. He shook his head and slapped his knee as he had in years past when he heard a good one. I nailed the punchline, and he was it. Playing a joke on Daddy all in fun was a throwback to happier times.

When I crept to the kitchen to start the coffee the next morning, I sensed a pronounced brightness coming from the window. I squinted, amazed. The entire yard was covered in a layer of white. Over an inch of snow topped the birdbath, confirming what Daddy knew all along. Alone in the kitchen, a catch in my throat, I saw that the joke was on me.

Daddy, Jane, and I toured two senior apartments a few miles from the Wisconsin border the next day. Daddy had been cordial enough to the sales staff, but he wasn't taking charge or asking the kind of questions I expected from him, ones about safety and cost and contracts. We bundled up for an evening meal at a soup and sandwich chain at the mall. As Daddy and I walked arm in arm in the brisk night air, I asked a question that came out of the blue, "Daddy, what's your favorite season?"

He said without faltering, "Oh, let's see. I think autumn." I replied that I loved autumn, too, and watched the chilly vapor from our conversation evaporate before my eyes.

After our meal, we strolled into a department store stuffed with Christmas decor to search for a new jacket for Daddy. Jane was tired of looking at the one he had been wearing for years. Or was she tired of the man wrapped inside, the one with the fading memory, the one who had stopped tickling her funny bone, nuzzling her neck? The one who couldn't manage without consulting the small bits of paper he kept in his shirt pockets and dresser drawers, clipped to the car visor and stuffed in the glove compartment.

As we searched the racks for XLTs, we came up short. Jane wasn't ready to admit that a simpler size would suffice now that Daddy was little more than bones and skin. In the meantime, I found a velour pullover in a deep jewel tone. "Daddy?" I asked as I held it up for him to see. He towered among shirt racks filled for the holiday season as "I'll Be Home for Christmas" crooned in the air.

Daddy nodded and reached for the hem of his sweater. What was he doing? My initial reaction was to usher him to the dressing room. Something stopped me. In seconds, Daddy had stripped down to his ribbed tank. I fumbled to get the shirt off the hanger and handed it over. He slipped on the pullover and poked his arms through. A perfect fit. I stood motionless and savored his rose petal skin, his tousled hair, and how good he looked in teal. "May I treat you, Daddy?" He laughed and nodded, looking pleased and fragile.

On the last afternoon of that visit, I sat in Daddy's chair in the living room reading a book, Paulette Jiles' *News of the World*. The historical fiction took place in Texas and encompassed a geography that Daddy and I knew well. Jiles' story and her writing style warmed my depths. My old dad would have loved the story. My new dad wasn't reading books anymore.

Daddy came in without speaking and lowered himself onto the dainty floral settee, a piece of furniture too squat and small for his long limbs. I had never seen him sit there before. Was it because I was in his chair? "Daddy, let me take that seat!" I offered as I took to standing. He waved me away and stretched out with his head on one armrest and his knees bent over the other. His calves and feet dangled in comic relief while his arms folded across his middle, his body unmoving on the upholstered blossoms supporting him. He closed his eyes and slept for over an hour. Had I ever seen my father asleep? A memory nudged me—Daddy napping in his recliner with the *Clarksdale Press Register* dropped to his chest. He had little time for rest in those days, I remembered. I didn't say a word but kept spying on Daddy, sensing that something was off kilter. A public nap on a miniature loveseat? That was odd. I fretted to myself but never told a soul.

I departed for home the next day, happy that Ellie would arrive on my heels to continue pushing Daddy gently toward change, encouraging him to adjust to a new way of living, just like he had started teaching us to do when we were five and three.

part three: reckon

a woman's hymn

she carries the weight of the world
bearer of water of custom of men
her creative powers shine in the eyes of the young
and she writes songs to heal sorrows born by gain

she gathers the dirty laundry
soaks it in vats of forgiveness
speaks when the occasion demands
or stands silent or wails

like her sisters, she arrives full-hearted each morning
ready again to hold the world together
with warm water and a drying towel

she reaches toward understanding the languages
of land and sky and sea
and sings in translation

thirty-four

I woke with a neck crick and blurry vision, the alarm on my phone pulsing the early hour. Where was I? The underside of the dining room table reminded me as I pulled Daddy's back pillow out from under my head. The grandfather clock had chimed on the hour and half-hour throughout the night, invoking the ghostly effects of *The Christmas Carol* when the Spirits visited one by one. Had I dreamed? I doubted it.

I listened for signs of life, heard none, and turned onto my back for a few deep breaths. *May I be healthy, may I be happy, may I be safe. May my life be filled with ease and freedom. May my thoughts and actions contribute to peace and happiness in the world.*[56] On slower mornings, I would loll in place and expand my prayer to the kids, to Trish, and sometimes to my entire circle of family and friends and then to all beings. This was not that morning. My inner voice shifted. *Rise and shine, dear heart,* my cheerleader nudged with a perkiness I needed. *Let's do this.*

I filled the tea kettle, pulled out the French press, and slipped into the downstairs half-bath to make ready. Soon Ellie and I were in Daddy's car driving to the hospital to see him before the surgery. Ellie would catch a rideshare shortly after for a mid-morning flight back to Houston. Jane would arrive at the hospital later with Nina. Traffic was light on this Monday of Thanksgiving week, the sky above still dim, city lights weak against the morning's gloom. My memory is wiped clean of what happened next. I don't remember parking, walking the tunnel to the lobby, finding Daddy's room. None of it. I can imagine Daddy on a gurney being rolled away from us, but that is all. My brain did not transcribe the parting. Had he already gone under? Had I kissed him goodbye? Said "I love you?" All I know is that

---

[56] Metta (lovingkindness) meditation; used to develop compassion toward all beings, including self

one minute Ellie was there and then she was gone. I had been ushered to the Neuro-surgical ICU Waiting Room. The conveyor belt of the medical industrial complex cruised on, unaware of a daughter's witnessing of her father's identity shrunk to a barcode on a wrist band. The amalgamation of processes and procedures and prophecies gave me no choice but to hold on for what Paul Harvey had coined as "the rest of the story."[57]

After hours of anticipation, the surgeon, a youthful, ruddy-skinned man, appeared in the waiting room, a space designed with partitions that allowed several families to commandeer space for themselves. "Are you the Fabriz family?" he asked. Jane and Nina sat with me now. We all nodded.

Dr. Brand invited us to join him at the computer station near the coffee machine. He took the lone swivel chair and faced the monitor where an image of Daddy's brain suddenly appeared. Behind his back, I took photos of the screen to send to Ellie later. "See this?" Dr. Brand traced concentric shadows that indicated more cancer than had been visible in the MRI the day before, damage the surgery had been unable to touch.

Dr. Brand murmured, "Let's see how he does." Whatever that meant. See how he does with a chiseled skull? a partial brain? cognitive decline on top of that? It was hard to take the doctor seriously in his grey sweats and backward-turned University of Minnesota Health baseball cap. Most hospital staff were wearing their UM merch, gearing up for the big football rivalry, a holiday tradition. I learned from one of the floor nurses that the Wisconsin Badgers vs. Minnesota Gophers game was scheduled for the impending Thanksgiving weekend and would be played in the stadium adjacent to the hospital. Minnesota would go down in a stunning defeat: 31-0, a loss I would likely never forget.

I either didn't or couldn't process the news we'd been given. Over the past eleven months, Daddy's diagnosis had morphed from mild cognitive decline due to Alzheimer's disease to inoperable brain cancer, discovered only after the surgeon opened his skull. What happened next was anybody's guess, but any guess wouldn't be good.

Daddy's day nurse, a retired army vet, had counseled me early that "nobody sleeps in ICU" and that my best bet was to head home at night for

---

[57] Paul Harvey hosted a radio program from 1952 to 2008 called *The Rest of the Story*, which employed Chekhovian twists. The stories were redemptive and hopeful in nature.

a shower, a meal, and a good night of rest. After a long day of sitting by my unresponsive father, I followed the suggestion without question, returning to Moss Road in Daddy's car. Nina had already deposited an exhausted Jane back home. Ellie and I agreed by text to talk again the next day after the doctors' rounds.

I became an automaton. A Vulcan like Spock. I sent my emotions to an inner sanctum for safekeeping and waited for someone to feed me my lines. I watched for an escape hatch like cornered prey. Metaphors unleashed in bad combinations as I tried to get at what was happening inside me. All the while, a wicked plot twist left Daddy strapped to a hospital bed with his head wrapped like a mummy.

I rose early the next morning, preempting the morning rush hour to be in Daddy's room by seven. As time went on, I translated "nobody sleeps in ICU" to "let us do our jobs" and "you're not needed here." Had the nurse been speaking code? Did he know that I should be resting up? Had there been a bet made on how many days we'd be around?

Like a private investigator, I buzzed from hall to hall, trying to learn the language of ICU. Could I speak to the nurses at the station or should I not? Could I expect the doctors to seek me out or was I luckless if they made their unpredictable rounds when I slipped out to fill my water bottle or to visit the women's room or to make a call? And which doctor did what and why and for whom? How did Daddy's advanced care directive, the one that was on file with his primary care doctor but not available to the network hospital, fit into the script? We were sent scrambling to get a copy faxed from his PCP to the care team before Thanksgiving, hoping it would land in the right hands. I took down notes about all that was unclear, unexplained, and inaccessible, and imagined lodging complaints when all this was over. I hoarded business cards with a huff. I shouldn't be made to feel like a dimwit at the bedside of what was coming into focus as a dying man. I decided that my job was to pay attention. What else was there to do but that?

During certain procedures, the nurses invited me to leave Daddy in their capable hands. I relented. Other families came and went from the ICU waiting room, some in a soul-spinning u-turn and others lingering, like the family who after two days received the final announcement from a teenage girl who slinked in, flapping the hem of her pink sweater. "She died," the girl mumbled, as numbly as she might report the weather. *It's sunny. It's cold. She died.* After murmurs of plans and the gathering of outerwear, the room emptied for the next wave.

Odd contrasts abounded. A wall-mounted television screen lit up with the anticipated Ellen Degeneres interview with Barbara Streisand while a blue-headed teen played a first-person shooter game that splatted monster flesh into view from the same computer monitor the doctor had used to show us the explosions of cancer on Daddy's brain.

∞

thirty-five

Thirty-six hours after Daddy's surgery, on the evening of the second day in the neuro-surgical ICU, Jane and I left the hospital discouraged. Daddy's eyes fluttered then shut, and his body went dormant. His breathing was labored after the removal of the ventilator, and his head was still eighty-percent bandaged. We returned home before the darkness set in.

Jane took to bed, and I slunk to the basement to keep going through Daddy's stuff. Whether he liked it or not, downsizing meant tackling all that Daddy had collected, dare I say hoarded, over the years. In a ferocious squall of unforecast emotions, I tossed old magazines, files from the '60s, '70s, and '80s, defunct insurance policies, owner's manuals from appliances long gone, and a four-inch stack of printed obituaries of his contemporaries that we later learned had been cross-referenced in his extensive address file. When I came across an artifact worth investigating, I slipped it into a large envelope for later. Little more than the need for mindless distraction egged me on.

By some miracle, in my frenzy, I found two undeniable treasures. The first was a small spiral notebook that contained a handwritten catalog of our grandfather's gun collection. I felt like a weary prospector who had finally struck gold and texted an immediate picture to Ellie. The thought of the guns had weighed heavy for months as she and I knew from our experience of packing them into the storage unit that we would eventually be the eligible parties left to determine their fate.

The second was from a bottom shelf—an old gift box with a blue floral cover labeled in Daddy's handwriting: 1971 Vacation. Inside was evidence of his meticulous planning and the exhaustive itinerary, all plotted on the map that he and I had passed forward and back from Clarksdale to the Pacific and home again.

My heart clenched as I read the pasted labels he had added along the map route, all starting with "Left Clarksdale 5/27/71" and "1968 Chevrolet station wagon pulling Apache Buffalo tent trailer" and another label nearby held a blue ink arrow pointing at Clarksdale that said "Start and end." His recordkeeping would have impressed any journalist. I traced my finger along the ballpoint loops Daddy had drawn on the map to indicate our tracks.

I searched the ink circles, that looked like links of infinity signs, for the exact location of my desert epiphany. Where had my faith been crushed by the blow of the diary epilogue? The map was empty of signs. I thought about how the news of Anne Frank's death rattled me then. I held to the belief that heaven was a construct, not a place. So what would happen to Daddy? I wasn't ready to contend with an answer to that yet.

Fatigue descended. I repacked the Vacation '71 box, hugged it close to my heart, and trudged the two flights of stairs to bed. The master bedroom shared a wall with the guest room, so eavesdropping was easy even when unintentional. Jane had a habit of listening to a late night call-in show on a local station. Usually, radio voices vibrated into the guest room. I had learned to bring headphones and earplugs to tune out the chatter. This night all was silent nextdoor.

I thought back to the chain of events of the past weeks. Would Daddy's last words be the pre-surgery garble impossible to translate? We must have looked ridiculous as we nodded and pointed and smiled and patted his arm and assured him that he would be fine, that he would have the surgery and that afterward everything would go back to the way it was. We humans like to think it will, and we even pretend it does—for months, for decades, sometimes for centuries. If only we paid attention to the signals. Fires come and smoke follows. Dreams distress sleep. A headache erupts. A basement empties of a recorded lifetime: pay stubs from an entire career neatly packaged in annual bundles, generations of photographs, mute moments that speak of little but posed positions and awkward angles. An occasional surprise—the rejection letter, the political cartoon torn from a newspaper, the divorce decree, inklings of upheaval. Was Daddy storing his losses in all that stuff?

At 10:18 P.M. within minutes of my head hitting the pillow, my cell phone lit up. A local area code. "Apologies for the late call. I'm the ICU doctor, calling about Leo. Breathing trouble…needs a respirator…wanted you to know." Every inch of me went numb. I knew what Daddy's advance directive said and was an ardent supporter of living wills, but Ellie was in Houston. I was alone with Jane, exhausted, and in no shape to argue. All I could reply was "Thank you." and "Goodbye."

"Jane?" I stood at her door in my black leggings and sweatshirt. "That was the ICU doctor. Daddy needs the respirator." Her hand flew to her mouth. I moved toward her and put my hand on her shoulder. "It doesn't sound good, but let's try to get some sleep."

Not more than three minutes later, Jane knocked on the wall that separated us. "Sharon? Sharon!" I pulled myself up to attention and took heavy-footed steps into the hallway.

Jane was sitting on the side of the bed, clinging to the white comforter, holding it up to her chin. "Would you stay in here with me tonight?" Her voice sounded thin and helpless. "I don't think I'll be able to sleep. I'm so scared."

I crept over to Daddy's side of the bed and turned down the covers, feeling mortification deep in my bones. My head rested on Daddy's pillow. I stared at the ceiling. My presence revived Jane. She chattered on and on. We would have to get some more cereal tomorrow and a couple bananas. Did I mind if she left the light on? What about the radio?

"Whatever you need, Jane. I'll be fine." I covered my head with the quilt to dim my senses. The image of my body covered by a white comforter was not lost on me. I sniffed at the sheets for signs of life.

I was up early the next morning and off again to Room 321. Jane would come later with Nina after they toured a senior living complex with assisted living and memory care options. I pulled a chair close to Daddy's bed and settled there with my digital reader, phone, and water bottle. Ventilator in place, Daddy was buried under the techno-wiz that kept his heart beating. Where was he now, I wondered. Had his mind traveled to the Outer Banks or the Grand Canyon? Maybe he had come upon the sheer rock wall above the cave at Blanchard Springs where he had taken a snapshot, the station wagon front and center, tent strapped to the top, his wife and girls inside primed for adventure.[58]

I shifted between reading to Daddy from *The Call of the Wild*, a Jack London favorite of ours, to playing tunes for him from my phone. I kept Glenn Miller's "Moonlight Sonata" on repeat, holding the receiver to his gauze-covered ear, hoping the waltz might sway his spirit toward whatever beauty he could perceive. But without his hearing aids and all of the bandages, how much was getting through?

Occasionally I rode the elevator to the main floor to assure myself that the real world was still functioning. How many days would Daddy and I have to endure the growling machines, numbing interruptions, the handmits, and tube feedings? Each doctor entered, unannounced, phone in one hand, chart in the other, and nodded at me before starting the routine inspection which seemed more abbreviated with each visit. They shouted at Daddy's wartorn, wrapped head, "Giva thumbs up! Giva thumbs up! Giva thumbs up!" and I wanted to throttle them. I begged to talk to a social worker, a chaplain, anybody who could help me see a softer side to this story. "They won't be back until Friday," Daddy's day nurse explained. "You know how it is on a holiday."

But I didn't know how it was on a holiday! All I wanted was to talk to somebody about my dad, for them to acknowledge something of the man he had been. Couldn't I explain that he was a lawman? a grandfather? a good guy? Was ICU a place absent of history?

Thanksgiving morning dawned. I woke up thinking about Nacimiento Road. The last five days had been nothing if not a journey of switchbacks and edges. I had made it through then, and I had to believe I would make it through now, sweaty palms and all. But what about Daddy?

"Good morning, Pappa." I said as I rubbed Daddy's dry, still forearm. Why had I called him pappa? I felt the softness of the 'p' and the 'ah'. Would life have been different had I called this man Pappa? Would I have been

[58] See cover.

different? Should I have been? Daddy's hands had been outfitted with the mitts again and some of his bandages had been removed. I thought about telling him that it was Thanksgiving Day, but didn't. Instead I spoke in quiet tones, "Thank you for being a good father. I love you, Daddy." I repeated the sentences several times over, hoping the message would arrive somewhere solid.

In what had become a familiar routine, I pulled a chair near him and placed my hand on his arm above his mitted hand. I filled the room with songs, "Great is Thy Faithfulness," "Home on the Range," "Que Sera Sera," a strange blend of melodies that filled the space with echoes from earlier times.

Midafternoon I made my way to the cafeteria, an airy eating space on the top floor that let in the sky. On the way there, I passed the window along the hallway that gave an unobstructed view of the vacant stadium, its colors of maroon and gold blaring, the big game inching nearer.

I'd never eaten a Thanksgiving dinner from a hospital cafeteria plate. I felt connected to all who had or were or would. I didn't expect to taste the turkey slice, green beans, and mashed potatoes, but I was determined to stay within my dietary limits now that I was three weeks into a month-long dietary purge to determine my food allergies and mitigate my migraines. Near the checkout counter, a serving bowl of Cholula hot sauce packets lifted my spirits. I took two. Memories returned of Daddy's daring migration to spicy foods when we moved to San Antonio. Our love of salsa and hot peppers bonded our palettes more tightly than Swedish meatballs did.

I spotted an empty table by a window and took a seat that faced outward toward the trees that indicated the Mississippi River. As hospital staff reveled in their complimentary holiday meal, the sights and sounds of mirth around me were hard to stomach.

I had lost the habit of saying grace over the years, but our family meal blessing landed on my tongue as naturally as the memories of Daddy rising early to sauté the onions and celery for Thanksgiving dressing. I bowed my head in dramatic fashion and spoke the words out loud, "Thank you, Father, for this food. In Jesus' name, Amen." I had been self-conscious over the years when my parents insisted on a public dinner blessing when we dined at restaurants. Today, I didn't care what people thought.

Daddy had given up the rite when he married Jane. During my annual visits, the awkward seconds preceding the start of a meal accentuated the absence of the prayer, an affront to all he and Momma had taught us about being grateful. Daddy had closed the door on the most fundamental of Christian rituals. Why?

I thought back to the conversation Daddy and I had at the Selby Grill over Veteran's Day, the way I had goaded him about not talking to Momma. Had our conversation ignited the poisons in his brain? My guilt grew as I watched dark clouds roll in west of the river. Why was I so quick to blame myself?

My plate clean, I lifted my tray and found the receptacle that receives such things. I grabbed the unopened packet of hot sauce before the tray disappeared and slipped the prize into my bag. Months later, I would remove it from my wallet and place it on my altar at home.

Daddy's state of health was not widely known. His social contacts had shrunk to neighbors, some younger F.B.I. colleagues, and a few distant relatives. His long-running lack of a church affiliation had preempted the presence of a minister or any congregants assigned to visit the infirmed. Most of all, his dearest of friends and associates were already dead, as evidenced by the weighty stack of obituaries found in his office.

We accepted only a handful of visitors, and one couple stood out from the rest. They arrived Thanksgiving afternoon, a kind, elderly couple, with Bibles in hand, who exuded the stance of what Momma called Believers. I hadn't seen Lois, a cousin of Grandma Sig's, since my grandmother's funeral. Today, she was joined by Paul, her second husband. I learned quickly that he was a retired minister.

Paul and Lois did not waste any time. They stood together at Daddy's bedside in a practiced pose that they would have performed often in their roles as pastor and pastor's wife. A piano sonata played from the only tv channel that I allowed, nature scenes layered with instrumentation, mellow and soothing. After I greeted them, I moved to the window and leaned against the ledge near the large portrait of my family that I had packed along. Trish, my children, their partners, and three dogs, had posed for a timed photograph last New Year's Eve. Our confluence of smiles steadied me here.

"May we pray?" Paul's shiny head bent over Daddy's encumbered body.

"Of course," I said as I dipped my head for what I guessed Daddy would have wanted.

Paul began to recite Psalm 23: "The Lord is my shepherd......yea though I walk through the valley of the shadow of death..." I raised my phone to take a photograph from my angle by the window then switched to the video camera thinking of Ellie. She would want to hear this. I held the camera steady. "...He restoreth my soul...." Did Dad's eyes open? Yes! He was looking at Paul as the minister continued, "Thou preparest a table before me....surely goodness and mercy shall follow me all the days of my life." In simultaneous motion, Daddy's mitted right hand lifted off the bed several inches and bobbed up and down as his eyes fluttered open and shut, open and shut. What? Daddy's in there! He's in there! My heart clamoured like it had when I was a girl and saw his car light's flash on the living room wall at dinner time. He's home! He's home! If this was to be Daddy's final act of volition, it was a dear one. "I'm listening," he may have been signaling. "Thank you." Whether he was addressing Paul or Father God or the Valley of the Shadow of Death did not matter. He was present in a holy communion I could not deny.

thirty-six

I don't want to think about the oval table, its softened edges as strategic as the chairs that swiveled and the wall color I remember as blue. I don't want to think about who was gathered there and who wasn't and why all that mattered. I don't want to think about the cell phone in the middle of the table on speaker so Ellie could be in the room for the family conference that had been scheduled and that would determine the fate of our father.

I don't want to think about the business cards, dealt to the family like hands for poker, from the Palliative Care Team that was perhaps known as the death squad by witty insiders who need to lighten things up every now and then. I don't want to think about the introductions in near whispers, the presentation of goals and the action plan, the protocol of circling the table for the yeses or nos, for the questions and concerns, for the round-up of cliches that must oxygenate ICU—*a dire prognosis, for the best, lived a long life, fulfilling his wishes, the Lord's will.*

Hardest to hear were the flat, devastated tones coming from Ellie through the phone line. She had taken a break from her brain injury patients to make this meeting. I was stranded on Pull the Plug Island with the secular family my father had married into - his wife, her daughter, her daughter's husband. How were we to reconcile the requirements of the day with the massive erasure of one human life? So much was far past possible now, the restitution of Daddy's memory, the sparkle in his eyes, simple breaths. The trust among us grew that day, when we knew as closest kin that we must sign the contract for one man's death. We were all tongue-tied and shaken by the inevitable separation that we had declared. Only one thing supplied me with courage—Ellie, my faithful sister, would arrive the next morning, and together, we would see this awful thing through.

The next morning, I woke to the foreknowledge of what was to come. Daddy would die on a crisp autumn Saturday at the age of 85 not far from where his life had begun. Were his mother and father awaiting his arrival in a heaven I refused to believe in? I would have to live with the mystery. Whatever soul remained in Daddy's battered body would be uncaged when the technology imposed on his systems was dismissed. My reluctance to face this reality shielded me from unacceptable loss.

I left the hospital long enough to fetch Ellie from the airport. The university neighborhood around the hospital had been transformed into a street party, students and alums outfitted in everything from maroon and gold Gopher wear to jester costumes reminiscent of Mardi Gras. The four-way stops that I had been able to breeze through all week were now major intersections of festivity. The irony did not amuse me.

Ellie threw her bag in the back and fell into the passenger seat. All was quiet until one of us said, "Well?" In the past five days, we had maintained a string of texts that wrapped around the block. Our combined shock and the ominous tasks that lay ahead kept our conversation light as we sped toward the hospital.

Here we were in the Twin Cities to put our father to rest. So many things had kept us apart in our lives, and Daddy's job had been the instigator for many. We hadn't been close like many sisters are, but we had a bond that was deep and understood. We both had faltered and forgiven each other's stumbles, we respected each other's ways as we got older, and we adhered to the dutiful-daughter handbook for just about everything. We had both gone into helping professions because one way or another, the design of the life that Daddy made for us gave us reasons to serve. We earned our own livings and operated as independently as any adult women in our situations did. We both tributed Daddy with teaching us those skills. In all these ways, we were good outcomes from his seed. Now we would step into our next task. To bury our father.

The road traffic had cleared by the time we arrived at the parking garage, all the revelers contained in the stadium. Ellie went directly to spend time with Daddy. Jane, Nina and her husband, and I waited with the young chaplain in the tomb of the waiting room.

The chaplain had appeared the day before, after the frustrating delay caused by the hospital's staff-friendly holiday scheduling. I shed genuine tears during our introductions, her tender handclasp reflecting a kinship I had not expected.

"You're a woman. A woman!" I squealed, covering my face as I spoke. "You have no idea what this means to me." I gave an abbreviated version of the reasons why. To have a female addressing my spiritual needs indicated the hospital's heart for inclusivity. After a brief summary of my life with Trish and my family's limited acceptance of us, she returned the favor by mentioning her wife, a generous reference meant to put me at even greater ease.

I excused myself from the rest of the waiting family for a brief stretch, needing a deep breath alone. The elevator took me to the cafeteria floor and the window that overlooked the stadium. Thousands of fans filled the stands. I stood there long enough to hear the crowd roar, but the points were not in the home team's favor.

I wandered back to ICU, contemplating Daddy's short future, cut now to an hour? maybe two? What had he already lost? His dance with Alzheimer's was cut short by brain cancer gone rampant. The surgery was either a ruse or divine intervention of the most expedient sort. Had anyone in their right mind expected him to recover? I had. My imagination reconstituted the able man he had been when I was a girl. I had idolized him then, and I wanted a full resurrection.

I peeked into Daddy's room and Ellie nodded, so I joined her. We spoke to Daddy for the last time. As I stood beside his bed, witnessing his powerlessness, I suddenly inhaled, raised my arms in the air, and in a burst of revival that arrived without thinking, I heard myself proclaim like a Southern country preacher in a voice that shook the air, "Be delivered into the arms of Jesus!" JEE-ZUSSS was more like it. I stepped back, knocked off balance by the spirited outburst. Where had that come from? I had been filled by a voice greater than my own. In my surprise, I nodded at Ellie and left for her to have a few more minutes alone with Daddy. My last words to him were a command from beyond me, that's all I knew.

Ellie came into the waiting room like a spent soldier, quietly acknowledging the circle of us. The chaplain maneuvered to a new seat nearer to me. Her arms stretched out like willow branches as she touched my knee with both her hands. Or maybe she was keeping me distracted while Sunny, Daddy's weekend nurse, wrestled the breathing tube from his trachea.

"It isn't pretty," Sunny had warned us in a sensitive paraphrase hours before. "You'll want to be in the waiting room until we get him situated." Later, Patrice told me that Sunny was right. It isn't pretty when all the bodily fluids release as a body dies.

I hadn't taken the time to fill in the blanks, connect the dots, decipher the code to its obvious conclusion. The words still land in me like slingshot stones: "until we get him situated." I simply agreed with the rest of the family to stay put in the waiting room until the breathing tube was removed.

The time came when Sunny swept open the waiting room door, her dark ponytail falling lopsided and her bangs all a panic, her skin baking in sweat. She exhaled the invitation for us to "go in now." Seeing her suppliant smile, I knew we'd been had. It hadn't been pretty, and we hadn't been with Daddy for the hardest part. May he forgive us for that.

We went into the room as millions have before us—into the room where a father lies dead, where all evidence of machinery has been removed and the sheets have been changed and some air freshener has been sprayed.

Daddy's body, still as stone, offered one comfort, the perfect "o" of his lips, room enough for his soul to slip through, the particles of his awareness now expelled into the surrounding air. His spirit would live on. At least for a while. We would see to that. But what would survive of him once his daughters were gone, too?

Ellie moaned and sobbed, bending close to Daddy as if she were sheltering him from the knowledge that she had to bear. Jane and Nina hugged and cried. I stood near the window by my family photograph a few feet away and started to sing. *When you walk through a storm, hold your head up high, and don't be afraid of the dark....*[59] Singing was the best I could do, and this time, I sang for myself.

---

[59] "You'll Never Walk Alone" is a show tune from the 1945 Rodgers and Hammerstein musical *Carousel*.

thirty-seven

Ellie offered to share her hotel room with me, since Nina was staying with Jane. I jumped at the chance. Near midnight, with a bed sheet over my head and computer in my lap, I stared from keyboard to shadowless screen and back again, repeating the pattern in a daze—sometimes typing, sometimes not.

"Entered into eternal rest" had been my sister's idea. "Died" was my preference, but I could adjust. As we reviewed the bones of Daddy's life, the limbs of his identity took shape, where he left tracks in the Land of 10,000 Lakes, the Mississippi Delta, and the Piney Woods of East Texas. I had scratched details into the small notebook that traveled with me almost everywhere, a habit developed as a way for me to keep up with myself and that I learned from Daddy.

Once a hint of daylight glowed around the edges of the blackout curtains, I crept out of the hotel room while Ellie still slept and took my laptop downstairs to the near-empty breakfast room. Tears dripped onto my sweatshirt as I finished the last couple paragraphs of what would become the public record of Daddy's life. The clanks of dinnerware and reports of the latest Presidential tweets were mournful accompaniments to my task as the room lightened to day.

I drifted to the business center. The monitor loomed large as my document came into focus. Once I returned to our room, I placed the printed draft on the laptop and asked Ellie to have a look. Had she read it? I hadn't a clue.

We descended the carpeted stairs, Jane, Nina, Ellie, and I, as the office came into view, the upstairs reserved for wakes and services and receptions. The faint mildew of the lower regions found my nose, reminding me of another basement, the one in the library where Daddy took us on Saturdays when we were "his girls."

Bilious wallpaper roses surrounded us. Southern Gothic came to mind. I looked into corners, expecting an apparition of Daddy to appear, William Faulkner style. I scrambled past the moment of supernatural possession and turned toward the pastel pew-length sofa and its curdled cushions. Gripping a folded piece of paper, I elbowed the arm rest to correct my posture and found a place for my feet on the colorless shag, intent on not crossing my legs, on maintaining a masculine posture.

Jane, the fresh and frail widow, landed beside me, her hip molding to mine, a position more common to sweeties on park benches, not us, not here. Nina sat in a ladderback nearby, and Ellie took the captain's chair near the door. A menacing desk of mahogany formed a staunch right angle with the arrangement, and its owner rounded its radius as if on cue. The Master of Ceremonies. "Good morning, ladies. I'm Lincoln."

The funeral director unbuttoned his black coat, uniform of his vocation. My attention swerved toward his name. Lincoln. Ping. "Four score and seven years ago." Ping. Springfield, Illinois, a road trip with Daddy. Ping. My birthday, the day President Lincoln had died. A throat cleared. I snapped back.

Lincoln held a black folder like a choir master. "This is a difficult time, but we need to go over a few things." His voice emitted a practiced reassurance as he removed his watch and set it on the desk blotter. "Get comfortable. This will take awhile." He sighed as if indicating that we could, too. We did and then leaned forward. Something told me this did not surprise him. As it turned out, little did.

I tried to keep the paper in my hand steady as we worked through the first hour of logistics—a checklist that began at the end with the lucky afternoon time slot he had nabbed at the National Cemetery for an honor burial three days hence. All else would be scheduled with that prized appointment in mind. Working our way backwards, that's what we were doing.

We answered Lincoln's questions about the music and pastor and visitation hours. He recommended caterers, and we settled on a color theme, the obvious red, white, and blue. Our simultaneous nods felt good, like we were doing something right. Yet we all seemed to be sinking.

"How about a picture?" he asked, both tentative and hopeful.

Ellie handed him an envelope containing a decades-old portrait of a distinguished man with an approachable smile and a twinkle in his eye. A man in his prime, we had all agreed. And the suit was blessedly blue.

Lincoln's hands folded into a child's prayerful pose. "Let's talk about the obituary."

I raised the paper I had been clutching and extended it toward him. He took it, wincing.

"Have an electronic copy available?"

Everyone turned toward me. I cleared my throat. "Of course. Is there somewhere I could log in?" Ellie and Nina, both tech savvy, shifted their hips and pulled out their phones, probably thankful for the break. I forced my shoulders back and tried to lengthen my spine. Jane sat mute, her arms limp at her side.

I followed Lincoln into an office space that might have been for a retail store or a plumbing business. But it wasn't. I was in the basement of a mortuary. Probably on the same level where Daddy was now on a slab, the makeup artist scheduled to do his face once the picture arrived. What about his carved skull? I shivered.

I pulled the rolling chair closer to the keyboard. Within minutes a digital file appeared on Lincoln's desktop, and we returned to the parlor, Lincoln unfolding the original I had handed him earlier.

I sat back down and brushed my hands over my thighs, crossing my legs despite my manly intentions.

"Alright. Just so we make sure we get it right before it goes to the papers, I'd like to read the obit out loud for your final approval. We have less than an hour if you want it published tomorrow. You're aware of the expense of publishing in both papers?" He scanned our slack expressions as our heads nodded.

Lincoln coughed and began: "Leo Fabriz, age 85, entered into eternal rest...." Suddenly every ear went on high alert. I folded my hands, focused my eyes on them, and forced my leg to stop shaking. My attempt at quantifying Daddy's life filled the airspace but with every word I felt I had betrayed the fullness of his purpose.

Lincoln's voice read on. "Leo held many church affiliations as his job moved him, his daughters, and his first wife, Miriam Tapper Fabriz, from place to-"

From beside me I felt a lurch, an elbow in my ribs, and a growl.

"What?" I asked flatly as I reared back. Loosening my scarf, I veered toward Jane.

"That's. Not. Ne-ces-sa-ry." Her arms now crossed, the widow clutched her forearms with opposing hands.

"What's not necessary?" My head snapped toward her as my hands slipped under my hips in hidden fists.

Jane broke her words into pieces for clear translation. "Men-tion-ing HER."

I rooted around for what to do next. My right hand flew to my chest and then in Ellie's direction. I shrieked at a volume that startled even me. "So, where did WE come from?"

Lincoln pushed back from his ergonomic chair and took leave like a stagehand. He pulled the office door closed behind him.

"Sharon," Ellie burst in, like a defensive lineman running interference. "Let me play devil's advocate here."

My voice scratched the air like a shrill cat. "I don't need you to be the devil's advocate!" Looking toward the captain's chair but not at Ellie, I muffled my anger and tried to sound scholarly. "Obituaries include historical details and the mother of Daddy's children is one of those details!" I yanked my scarf tight and a choking hush followed.

Time stopped long enough for me to grasp the odds: three against one. I hefted my right leg away from my left, pushed myself toward the edge, and planted my feet into a bullish pose. The only thing I could do was see how hard the other side wanted to fight. "I must insist that my mother's name appear in the obituary." Again dead air took over.

Jane tapped the face on her watch as her eyes bored into her daughter.

Nina's voice broke the silence. "Mom, can't you give on this one thing?" Her look, aimed at Jane, begged "Surrender!" Nina waited. Ellie waited. I waited.

The hush must have been too much for her. Jane's hands flew up like perturbed pigeons. "I don't like it." she squawked. "I don't like it at all!"

I waited a couple seconds for the deal to seal and then stretched upward, stepped over to the office door, and rapped a couple times. "Lincoln?" I said in my most demure of deliveries as I reached to open the door, "I think we've worked it out."

He must have been listening because the door opened before I let go of the knob. "Now then. Shall we go on?" he asked as he straightened his tie.

Once all was said and done, Ellie took the driver's seat in Daddy's car for the silent trip back to the house to drop off Jane and Nina. We spoke in efficient half-sentences and agreed on when to regroup.

Ellie and I returned to the hotel in silent mode, our marching orders in hand, knowing better than to discuss the events of the morning anytime soon. Once inside, we each claimed our bed as an office and started working through our agreed-upon tasks. As we calculated for the catering arrangements, our conversation escalated into an argument about who was more controlling. I had contended with the perpetual "do not disturb" sign Ellie insisted stay on the door to keep housekeeping at bay, and she had dealt with the reams of notes I had taken to keep track of what I was afraid I would forget, which was everything. We were worn to the bone.

"I couldn't do this without you," I finally conceded.

"We're in this together, " Ellie sighed.

We hugged with a strength of conviction that our obligation to be good daughters required us to be good sisters, too.

Days later while Jane and I were sitting alone recapping the viewing, the service, the mourners, the flowers and cards, she said, "I learned so much about your father that I didn't know."

I couldn't say a word. Yes, there was so much she would never know. Especially about Momma, the wife who wore the badge of F.B.I. wife with pride, cheer, and class. Who kept up appearances and learned the politics of survival in Southern society so far from her Minnesota home. Who was kind. Who contended with the chronic losses of her progressive neuromuscular disease without complaint. Who insisted on our respectful admiration of everything Daddy. Who received Daddy's twenty-year Special Agent pin because he told her she deserved it.

People can't be disappeared from each other by the swipe of a mouse or a backspacing frenzy. History may work that way, but not family, not the up-close-and-personal tie that bears the fingerprints of loss and the chromosomal couplings, incompatible or not. Truth does not dismiss its mothers.

If I could put odds on it, I would say that Jane never read the published obituary.

When Ellie submitted her version to the glossy FBI magazine, she extracted the sentence about Momma, eliminating her with an intention I am incapable of grasping.

thirty-eight

Ellie and I agreed that Paul was the singular choice to conduct the funeral. His presence at Daddy's bedside had been a gift of grace. We contacted him shortly after Daddy died to ask if he would lead the service.

Paul and Lois arrived on Moss Road bundled up, frigid air trailing behind them. Once their coats were stored, we all moved toward the dining room, the place I had slept on arrival. We took our places around the French Provincial table, Daddy's INSTRUCTIONS folder serving as our centerpiece. A few short months before, Ellie and I had stood with Daddy in the basement, circling to examine the folder and the future we hadn't seen coming.

The contents included a Planned Transitions portfolio that was thoroughly completed with Daddy's handwritten listings. Ellie and I had perused the booklet for relevant information. Two entries focused our attention. *Favorite literature or religious passage/verse* had been modified with cross outs and handwriting to read *Favorite religious doctrine*. Daddy had written on the lines provided, "Christian hope of resurrection and eternal life." Beneath that item was another that piqued my interest more: *Specific requests*. Three lines in Daddy's printed hand followed: *Reminder that this body is but a tent for my soul on the bivouac of life, and that death is life's next great adventure.* The poetic proclamation impressed me. Way to go, Daddy!

The documented evidence would come into play as we discussed the kind of service that we wanted. "We" quickly split into "I" and "I" and "I" as preferences became personal, the dining room table morphing into its own version of a contested borderland.

"What church do you attend, Jane?" Paul asked in complete sincerity.

"I don't." Jane answered flatly. She hadn't expected the question and had no intention to elaborate.

On one thing, Jane and I agreed. The service shouldn't be a religious one. Paul and Ellie exchanged concerned glances as I made a quantifiable observation. "Paul, Daddy didn't have a church affiliation and hadn't worshipped in public for thirty years. In my mind, that's an important consideration." Let Daddy's life speak for itself, I thought. There was plenty to say about who he had been. In a series of filmed interviews I had conducted with him when he was eighty, my final question related to words of wisdom he wanted to pass on to his great-grandchildren. He hesitated for a moment, rubbing his thumb and forefinger in a friction of thought. "Remember who you are," he answered. "That's important."

As relevant as the advice was to the life he had lived and how he had lived it, I kept the disclosure to myself. I was tired of fighting against other people's dogged pursuit of heaven. Ellie handed the Planned Transition booklet to Paul, pointing to the entry Daddy had made about his favorite religious doctrine. "You can keep this for now," she urged, pressing it into his hands. She wasn't going to play the devil's advocate card this time. Full out crusade was on her mind.

The meeting ended with a prayer that included a special appeal. "Bless Jane and keep her. Open her heart to the riches of Your glory." Her churchless affiliation must have instigated the petition for her soul. Paul was an evangelist; he wasn't going to give up that role until he reached the Pearly Gates himself. I would prepare for the inevitable, a gospel[60] funeral message courtesy the death of Daddy. The art of compromise forced my hand.

---

[60] the message concerning Christ, the kingdom of God, and salvation

∞

thirty-nine

Our morning schedule the day of the funeral was subdued. With more hotel rooms now reserved, I was sharing with Liz. Brad and Lara had a room of their own. Ellie now hosted her son Drew. The cousins had stayed out late at a pizza joint nearby, so Liz was deep under the covers well after sunrise. While she slept, I caught up on emails, reviewed my eulogy, and finally closed myself in the bathroom for a shower.

I unfolded a fresh washcloth, spread it on the counter, unzipped the makeup bag and pulled out everything I would need: moisturizer, eye cream, eyedrops, foundation, eye shadow, mascara—fully aware with every placement that I was preparing to put on my face for my father's funeral. At this time of year, my Scandinavian complexion was light as cream. Today, I looked paler than usual, tired. Tired of being considerate, sensible, neat.

I hoped my dress would fall around my frame in a way that at least made me look stately, not chubby, a word taken from the line of clothing I wore as a girl. I would spend hours looking through the Sears catalog, picking out my favorite fashions. "Only look at the Chubbies," Momma would remind me, and at that, I'd have to start from scratch.

The dress had arrived in Minnesota through a series of handoffs. Liz took the midnight train six hours from her mountain town to Sacramento where Trish picked her up and delivered her to the airport.

We had arranged for Liz to leave room enough in her pack for my dress, shoes, and tights. Trish rolled everything up together and tied the parcel with a ribbon. When I opened the bundle, inside was a card addressed to "Juniper." We had adopted terms of endearment on our camping trip to California seventeen years before. I was her Juniper and she was my Sugar Pine. Since I had the contents of the care package in the bathroom with me,

I opened the card. Inside was the loving support one partner gives another in a time of sorrow. Included was a half-sheet titled "A Prayer from Trish:"

May suffering come to an end. May differences be set aside. May common ground be found. May grieving occur without judgment. May this Peace come to you and your family.

I held the paper to my heart. May it be so, I whispered. May it be so. I still struggled with Trish's absence from this occasion. Yes, she was needed at her school. That was true. But we all knew the real reason she wasn't here. I hadn't pushed it. I didn't want Sharon-and-her-girlfriend to be the subject of side conversations, finger-pointing, and rejection. We'd had enough of that. Would Daddy have wanted Trish there? Maybe. Maybe not. He had been courteous at telephone distance as the years rolled on. He'd ask, "How's Trish?" and listen politely. "Tell her hello!" he'd add, and that would be that. He and Jane had never invited Trish to their home, and my trips to Minneapolis had always been solo, Trish's name mixed in conversations like a spicy element that could only be added in small doses.

After a hot shower and a quick blow dry, which I thought might urge Liz awake, I moisturized and put on my face, leaving the contents of my bag splayed on the washcloth. Momma had taught me the importance of putting on my face. "Make yourself presentable!" had been one of her hallmark phrases. She didn't leave her apartment without applying lipstick and fixing her hair. I knew she was already incanting prayers that today would go smoothly for Ellie and me. She was grieving, too.

I hung the damp towel on a hook and creaked the door open to let out the steam.

Liz was already up, standing at the window against a perfect, blue sky. The flag in the distance flew flat as a postcard. I joined her and together we watched the last stubborn leaves tumble from the trees near the parking lot.

"The dress looks nice, Mom." Liz said as she sipped her coffee, pointing to a cup for me on the nightstand.

"You know just what I needed to hear." I answered, toasting my cup to hers. The dress, a simple design of navy fabric that fell in soft folds, had served me in my last official act as a teacher and would serve me this day of endings, too.

As soon as Liz was dressed, we met Brad and Lara downstairs for breakfast. Liz had opted out of being a pallbearer, but Brad and Ellie's son Drew would serve. Seeing Brad in his suit, his lanky frame outfitted for his grandfather's funeral, made my heart squeeze hard.

"Hi, Mom, how ya doin'?" Brad asked as he offered the first of many hugs we would share that day.

The riffs on love for my children could expand into volumes. They had been patient with my many incarnations and loyal to me despite my shortcomings. My son and daughter had found their ways to alternate lives in a yin yang of urban and rural, academic and organic, analytic and intuitive. Both had adopted the politics of caring and a community-mindedness that made me proud. These young adults whom I treasured had met with inconveniences major and minor to be here, and their sacrifices were not lost on me.

Soon Ellie and Drew entered and the first hour of our day began with a happy reunion. Ellie's daughter and her three children were not able to travel from Houston and their absence suddenly was made real. We were a scattered clan, and the desire to reassemble had never felt stronger.

forty

The world fluttered on as the first day of December had us parking Daddy's car in the lot of the funeral home where his casket and its soulless contents waited for the formalities to begin.

During the final visitation, Lincoln took me aside. "I've already talked to your sister and Jane, but I wanted to let you know that because of your father's height, before we close the casket, we will have to tip his upper body backward so that we can bend his legs for a better fit." He wasn't asking permission. I had already detached from the body in the casket and from the cosmetically-ravaged face that did not reflect my father's heredity or his good humor. How could they have gotten him so wrong? All of his Leo-ness had been lost to the artless reconstruction of strangers. I advised Brad and Liz not to view the distortion of Daddy, a visage undeserving of memory.

I considered Lincoln's explanation. Daddy would be forever tilted downhill, legs bent in a pose he probably loved as a boy on summer days down by the river. "Makes sense," I replied, like this was the most normal conversation in the world. Pulling like a needy puppy, I caught the edge of Lincoln's black suit coat. "I want to apologize for my emotional outburst in the meeting the other day. I know I lost it."

He leaned in with the kind of one-sided grin that reminded me of Daddy and whispered, "Happens all the time."

A hundred or so chairs had been set up in two sections split by a center aisle. From our location, the pump of the organ's foot pedals added off-kilter clunks to the hum of chords just loud enough to bury the whispers of guests beneath "God Bless America," "The Navy Hymn," and a handful of standards that we had approved. Both Ellie and I unseated ourselves whenever we spotted a second cousin or a neighbor or a church member we recalled from earlier decades. The bodies had changed, but the eyes and the voices held whiffs of childhood memories that secured my place in time. These guests had known the man I would be remembering today.

After Paul opened the service with a welcome and a prayer in Jesus name, we daughters commenced to speak. Nina took the podium first, sharing details of the early years when her mother and Daddy had married. "Leo and I were both only children, and that bonded us." Nina was the local daughter-on-call and faithful celebrant of all things Jane and Leo for the thirty years of their marriage. The series of vignettes she shared evidenced her love for Daddy. They had learned how to pal around and appreciated each other's intelligent wit. The truth is, she knew the man Daddy had become in the last thirty years better than I did.

Ellie spoke next. She and I hadn't discussed what we planned to say. She stood, composed, as she thanked those in attendance and then began. "When going through some things in Dad's drawer, I found....a small Bible, a New Testament and Psalms that Dad had given to his father on his dad's fiftieth birthday in 1949, according to the inscription written inside."

Ellie stopped in a dramatic pause, then continued, "Another inscription shows that in 1972, my grandmother gave that same little New Testament and Psalms back to my dad on his fortieth birthday."

I breathed in the quiet of that moment, consoled by the rise and fall of my sister's voice, then snapped back and realized I had missed some of what Ellie had said. Her voice had slowed and softened. She had her hand at her heart. "...Dad has that Bible now in his chest pocket." With that, she looked toward the coffin, now closed and draped in a flag.

As Ellie returned to her seat, I took another deep breath, rose from mine and stopped to offer hugs to Jane, Nina, and Ellie. At the podium, I planted my feet in mountain pose and followed the notes I had added to my double-spaced, 14-font script. *Stand quietly, breathe deeply, look outward and count to ten.* This advice I had received from Patrice. She had trained as a celebrant, and I trusted her counsel. She had also cautioned me against glorifying Daddy. Nobody's perfect, she had reminded me. Don't be sappy.

With one more inhale, I began. "...Of all the things that Daddy provided to support me through the passages of my life—and there have been many—his talent for finding humor in the hardest of situations is a survival skill that has helped me find lightness in even the heaviest of loads."

"As Ellie and I, distraught and tired, reviewed Daddy's meticulous memorial planning instructions, we found an entry that was most curious. In what clothing did he want to be buried? We squinted at his scribbling: *silk pajamas and a white smoking jacket*. Laughter erupted just like it had when we read that detail. After the room quieted, I continued with a giggle, "...exactly what he had expected from us, we're sure." I went on to describe the 1971 Camping Trip box I had found earlier in the week and the conclusions that could be drawn from the evidence inside along with my experience as a fellow traveler on that mind-expanding trip to California.

"Over the course of the thousands of miles we traveled, I read like crazy....I grew into new ways of thinking and feeling." I let that sentence wash over me, thankful that I could credit Daddy with such powerful outcomes. "...Daddy created the conditions for me to experience a reality that was much bigger than I could have ever imagined." It was true, without Daddy, my childhood would not have been what it was, multiple experiences of movement, challenge, and change. "...He offered the possibility that the world exists not for me to ignore or fear, but for me to explore and befriend." Who would I have become without Daddy's unflinching entrance into the unknown? His courage to open new doors and acquire skills of belonging in new places and times had both frustrated and guided me.

Daddy spent hours of his life in the driver's seat as a family man, an F.B.I. agent in rural territory, and most recently as an intrepid chauffeur for Jane. "...Daddy's love of driving is an apt metaphor for how he lived his life. He understood the rules of the road, used reliable maps to plot his way, preferred the scenic route, and was always ready to stop for ice cream.... Thank you all for being here today to celebrate Daddy's life with us as he loosens his grip on the steering wheel and learns how to fly."

As I took my seat, I felt shame at my tearless delivery. What might people think about a daughter who doesn't cry, not once, during the eulogy for her father? Either I couldn't cry or wouldn't. Which? I wondered. Brad patted me on one shoulder and Liz on the other. Having them in the seats behind me felt good, like protections from a storm of emotions yet to arrive.

Ellie's son took the podium and his 6'7" physique brought Daddy's presence back into the air space like nothing else could. Drew read from a small journal that my father had given him, a collection of reflections meant to shorten the distance between them, a grandfather and his youngest grandson. Something in the timber of Drew's voice drew a droplet to my eye.

Paul spoke next. My memory recorded little of his sermon about the new man Leo had become, perfected in Christ, rematerialized with the heavenly multitudes by the grace of God, joined with his mother and father and all Christian brethren for eternity. I instead pictured Daddy as a boy of ten, a final bike ride to the park, a climb down onto the granite ledge carved by eons, a careful trek behind the falls, the spilling splash and foam and bubble raucous in its escape from gravity, its aerated pursuit of mystery, its betweenness of being. I would hold my image of Daddy there, behind the wall of water, where all becomes tumble and motion and drift.

The night that followed offered a respite from the rigors of a day that included a reception, drive to the cemetery, the honors burial, and a special dinner for family and friends. Ray, who flew in unexpectedly to pay his respects and jump on the chance to see both our children at once, scored some pricey wine and a corkscrew. We held true to our co-parenting promise, and this moment reflected that vow. People can choose to communicate, to find a way. Actions spoke louder than words. Brad, Lara, and Liz perched on the queen beds of the hotel room as Liz filled the paper cups to their rims. "Here's to Daddy!" I toasted, looking upward.

As the hour crept toward midnight, we talked of many things, of how great it was that Daddy never had to hand over his car keys; he had driven Jane and Ellie to dinner the night before he was hospitalized. We talked of Trish's absence and why she should have been here. We talked of divorces and damages done and of discoveries incumbent on the losses we had each suffered. In our circular trust, we each drew a card from a divination deck that Lara had packed along. The reading was founded on the simple question: *What's next?* We tossed around insights and connections from our draws. For a few precious hours, we synced our hearts and sunk into the softness of remembering who we were.

The children flew out the next day while Ellie and I remained to help with the aftermath. We wrote thank you cards and made a list with Nina of all that we needed to do to shutter Daddy's life. Jane insisted that we clean out Daddy's closet and bureau before we departed. It was then that I found the teal shirt, my impromptu Veteran's Day purchase, its tags still attached.

On the day of departure from St. Paul, Ellie and I agreed to stop at the cemetery on the way to the airport, since they were near neighbors.

"Can you believe that a month ago we were here with Daddy on his birthday?" Ellie reminded me.

I answered with a solemn "I know." The wild timeline of events was settling into place.

From the curving interior road that wove through the cemetery grounds, we spotted Daddy's new address. A freshly bulldozed row of plots rumpled the edge of acres upon acres of white marble markers, rows bending with the landscape and held in neat precision by a heft of heroes.

Our coats bundled around us, we walked the uneven ground that was hardening under the late autumn freeze. Ellie and I had never held each other like this before, clutching each other's waists, an unexpected clinging to what was left of our father. When we were children, Grandma Sig had reminded us many times that siblings are technically the closest of relations, sourced from the same blood, a shared inheritance. Ellie wept and I imploded as we reached the cardboard placard that would one day be replaced with a headstone mirroring thousands of veterans' graves.

A rumble disrupted our grief, and we turned to see. An airplane lifted in flawless wonder—and soon another. Daddy's grave faced the departure runway, the promise of far destinations in view.

forty-one

My year of marathon absences from home had to be extended one more time. I would fly not to Calfornia, but directly to Houston for a long-planned trip to see Momma for her eighty-fifth birthday. As I recounted the events of the past days, she perseverated on the death of her own father sixty years before. All my losses were made small in the shadow of her memory. I would have to bear the disappearance of Daddy alone. The anticipation of a full return to Trish and Mocha would be the best gift the holiday season could give. My body cried deeply for home.

I arrived back in Sacramento just in time to create a winter holiday vibe, adding Glinda, the Good Witch of the South, to the roof of the stable in the nativity scene. Nostalgia led me back to the day I had driven myself to the afternoon matinee of *The Wizard of Oz* during its thirty-fifth anniversary theater run back when I was sixteen. I was in Minneapolis during a summer visit, and Grandma trusted me with her car, a classic 1963 Ford Fairlane in fine condition. When she handed me the car keys and a written set of directions to the theater, I beamed.

The film had been something of a television holiday classic in the 1960s, and I had seen the movie several times either on Grandma's small black-and-white television when we visited her at Christmastime or at home on our small black-and-white set. Daddy was not about to spring for a color TV until prices came down.

I bought a matinee ticket and found a seat front and center with plenty of empty space around me. The opening farm scene exploded onto the screen and the larger-than-life faces took on new meaning as the story reintroduced itself. The entire theater rumbled with the force of the tornado, and the transformation of Almira Gulch on her bicycle into the Wicked Witch on her broom was as upsetting as ever. When the airborne farmhouse landed,

Dorothy picked up Toto and opened the door onto a polychromatic scene: a curving bridge over a sapphire brook filled with ivy green lily pads near the spiraling start of the unmistakably yellow brick road. I gasped like a child. Colors?! My eyes filled with tears.

The spectacle was a brilliant surprise. The blue gingham of Dorothy's dress, the green skin of the Wicked Witch, the poofy pinkness of Glinda, the fiery poppies, the emerald of Oz all fulfilled a wish I hadn't known to make. The grayscale television sets kept something from me that I hadn't thought to imagine. The moment belonged among intimate others that took me off guard and startled me into a new way of seeing, like the glaring truth of my first day of school and that desert moment when I lost faith in heaven. My worldview whirled with one part *The Wizard of Oz*, one part *The Diary of a Young Girl*, and one part The Golden Rule in a trinity of grace that was mine alone.

My creative streak continued as I dug through the Christmas ornaments. To the nativity scene, I added Hermy, the Misfit Elf from *Rudolph the Red-Nosed Reindeer*, my favorite holiday animation and possibly the gayest holiday story of its age. I nestled a small blown-glass red devil in the corner of the stable and leaned a Peace Activist pin against the manger close to the open arms of Baby Jesus. In a final act of playfulness, I adhered a red retro tree-topper to the teal buddha head on the top of the bookcase. Whatever had been loosened in me felt good.

forty-two

I hunched in the back seat of the rideshare and fidgeted with my phone. "Jane? I'm on my way."

The maroon Escape sizzled through the icy, snow-piled streets of south Minneapolis finally arriving in northeast St. Paul. Why would anyone fly from California to Minnesota in February? Aside from the fact that the Superbowl had just been hosted by the Twin Cities, no reasonable answer came to mind. But then, life was not reasonable anymore than it was fair. My job was to console the new widow and further diminish my father's belongings so that Jane could put her house on the market.

The turn into the driveway of the neat, two-story revealed from the porch a coatless, feeble woman waving like royalty. As the toasty cab idled, I eyed the scene like a character in an English play whose generous intentions eventually sour into complicity. The rideshare vanished as my knee boots marched down the shoveled path to the parted door, my compact suitcase bumping behind me.

"Phew!" I tried to sound pert. Heat blasted my face as I parked my bag against the wall. "I made it."

A side hug ensued with the obligatory pats, then Jane mumbled something as she moved toward the floral settee, the one that held my secret memory of Daddy's afternoon fatigue. I hung my puffy black coat on a wooden hanger that I knew had held Daddy's leather jacket until the day we piled it in the stack for the Goodwill along with the teal pullover he had publicly modeled at the mall. I wrapped my scarf around the neck of the hanger and pulled it like a noose; a dramatized ugh. I bent and unzipped my boots, laughing as I spoke to them. "You've gotten pretty used to this, huh?"

Only later did I pull the boots back on to walk to the neighborhood grocery for the items that would ease my stay: coffee, almond milk, eggs, olive oil, salsa. An avocado if I were lucky. I was still conscious of my health, trying to sync my rhythms and control what I could. I wanted to feed myself good stuff, body, mind and spirit included.

The next morning, Jane and I each served ourselves: coffee and eggs with salsa for me and lactose free milk over puffed rice for Jane. We ate from our seats in the living room. I took Daddy's chair.

Jane couldn't help but speak between bites. "Your father made life hell for me the last five years. crunch. Just hell! crunch. He didn't want to get rid of anything. crunch. Ever! crunch. I would ask him and ask him go through all that crap, and he just wouldn't do it. crunch. And he didn't want me down there. crunch. If we were down there together, crunch, he would stick closer to me than when we made love, crunch, and I'm not kidding you. crunch. And when are you girls going to get those storage units cleaned out? crunch. I don't want to have to keep paying the rent on them!" crunch. crunch. crunch.

I gazed at my eggs and took small sips of coffee until her diatribe ended. "We're going to have everything cleaned out by the end of summer, Jane." I scooped a pile of eggs and salsa onto my fork and told myself to taste every bite. "That's what we all agreed."

Jane put her gnarled index finger up to her mouth. "I kept asking him what was in all the boxes, and he never could tell me. My estate, he would say. Family treasures, my assssss." She lifted her bowl and slurped, looking at me like I owed her an explanation.

"Well, Jane." The grandfather clock interrupted me and gonged seven times. "Here we are."

As she rose to her feet, in a more virtuous voice, Jane spoke. "Tell me again - what are we doing today?" and she tipped up her bowl one more time to make sure it was empty.

I had been a young mother when Daddy married Jane and moved into her house. She was sole proprietor, according to the pre-nup, and he was the caretaker. I had lived lifetimes in the past three decades, and I realized that my father had, too. His life with Jane was real and daily for thirty winters, springs, summers, and falls. My time with him over the past one-hundred-twenty seasons had been whittled to a few August days each year, augmented by phone calls, cards, and the occasional letter. His identity as a father existed now only in my memory and in the DNA of my sister and me, our children, her grandchildren. Even his surname would be buried soon. After my divorce, I had reclaimed my maiden name, determined to reattach to my family of origin, but my children had their father's family name. The Spanish surnames of Ellie's grandchildren would represent the future of our family line.

On the last day of my visit, before saying adieu to Moss Road forever, I lolled under the butterfly quilt, which I had grown to love. My hand reached for my phone and scrolled to the collection of photos I had taken during Daddy's week in ICU. They were getting in the way of my peace. The time was right to delete them, here in the place where I had slept on my father's side of the bed the night his life did not become his own. Daddy had disappeared from all but the stacked boxes in the basement. The house would hit the market in mere months. Jane was thrilled at the emptiness that surrounded her. All the vanishing set me packing for home.

∞

forty-three

A new June had arrived, and I imagined that grass now grew over Daddy's settled grave. I was scheduled to drive a rented Suburban to meet Ellie in St. Paul where we would contend with the contents of the storage units, the largest two of which Daddy had rented for almost thirty years since Grandma Sig sold the family home. I couldn't bring myself to calculate the thousands Daddy had invested in those holding cells.

We had peeked into the units during the firearms mission with Daddy the June before but were unable to step inside, so packed to the gills were they with the toppling towers of three generations. The third and most recent unit had been acquired just a year ago this very week with us at Daddy's side. For the guns.

Completing the waiting task would require me to drive nineteen hundred miles from California through Nevada, Wyoming, and South Dakota to the storage units whose keys I now possessed. I planned to extend my drive time to allow for visits to places made famous on Daddy's Viewfinder, a nifty slideshow gadget from the '50s. I had clicked through photographs of the Black Hills, Devil's Tower, and Badlands National Park dozens of times as a girl, dreaming of the day I could see those places for myself. So far, I had never been.

Before returning to the storage rooms, I trusted the road trip to lighten my resistance. The big sky would help prepare me to decipher what was worth keeping. If I was to serve as co-curator of the residual evidence of the Fabriz legacy, I needed to armor up with wide horizons.

I planned three nights of lodging in homestay private rooms offered through an online service, wanting the security of a host and the sense of being expected along the way. My food bag held what I had learned traveled well: nuts, avocados, rice cakes, apples, granola, protein bars. A cooler held kombucha, almond milk, and frozen bottles of water. Yes, I would succumb to fast food french fries. What's a road trip without them?

Driving through Wyoming was like reading pages by Annie Proulx or being on the set of a sweeping western. *Brokeback Mountain* came to mind. I hiked the path around Devil's Tower in a daze of wonder, stopped off at Deadwood for a hike to the top of the cemetery where its first sheriff, Seth Bullock, now rested in a lofty position that looked over the entire town. I toured the Black Hills, understanding at once why Sturgis, South Dakota, was a meeting place for motorcyclists each summer. I envied their wild leanings. Badlands National Park compared to nothing else I'd ever seen, erosion's sculptures drawing forth the creative powers of wind and time. Thunderstorms followed me east as rivulets rose into rivers. South of Mankato, Grandma Sig's childhood home, Google Maps sent me down a dirt road at sunset in the middle of nowhere. My persistence took me back to the highway where I saw what I had been diverted from: a vacant construction zone with not a worker in sight.

I entered the outskirts of Minneapolis near ten p.m. in light traffic, texting my lodging host that I was near. The freeway exit I needed was the same one I had used to get to the hospital months before. The first sidestreet led to the garage where I had parked Daddy's car on my daily trips to the ICU last November. One more turn, and I was near the banks of the Mississippi, the grand liquid motion that connected the North and South of my life.

∞

forty-four

The morning after my arrival in St. Paul, I met Ellie and my ten-year-old grandniece, Sophie, at the airport. Ellie would pick up a rental van the next day. This was Sophie's first trip to Minnesota, so we headed straight for Minnehaha Park, a must see on every visit. Sophie skipped toward the sound of thundering water. Ellie and I followed, taking our places beside Sophie on the bridge that arched over the falls. The creek did what it had done for centuries, dismantling, shape-shifting, announcing itself in resounding thunder as something new altogether. Then, in quick order, the fallen flow reclaimed form, found its banks, and moved on. From this geographic heart, my inheritance emerged as surrender, freefall, and recovery. The pull of these waters ran through my life, the silt settling like tea leaves, sealing my fate. This place foretold the story of my life.

While Sophie darted like a dragonfly from one view of the falls to the next, Ellie whispered an idea of what we should do next. I nodded in happy agreement. Today was not a day for working, no-sir-ree, as Daddy would say. Ellie and I were cooking up a surprise for Sophie, and we needed the dose of fun as much as she did.

I drove on instinct to the parking lot of a St. Paul community treasure. Como Park Zoo. As soon as Sophie spotted the carousel from the backseat window, she squealed. "Are we going here? For real?!"

Ellie laughed the way grandmothers do who are proud of themselves for their good ideas. "Maybe Aunt Sharon will go on a few rides with you," she joked.

"Are you kidding?" I answered. "I'm riding more than a few!"

Sophie bounced up and down on the car seat, her dark hair bobbing into her face. I remembered that kind of glee and decided to stick close to that wave of good energy. The power of play could not be underestimated.

We strolled the zoo first, and then raced toward the carnival. Ticket passes in hand, we sped straight for the roller coaster. Ellie followed, her phone already in camera mode. After repeating the ride three times, we circled the small park and rode almost every ride twice—Tilt-a-Whirl, carousel, bumper cars, and zipline included.

As we were about to leave, I suggested we try The Tornado, the ride by the gate that we had missed. Sophie and I laughed as we whirled, gravity pulling us against the metal hull. Ellie waved from the fence.

As our car slowed, I lifted my right leg out toward the ground to stop the compartment from spinning but miscalculated my strength. The force of the machine pulled my leg under and my knee twisted backward in a screwdriver of pain. A scream rose in my throat, but I didn't want to worry Sophie. I clutched the metal casing of the car and reduced my eruption to a quieter response. "Ouch! Ouch! Ouch!" I peeped. Somehow I unwound myself and stumbled toward the gate, not realizing I was as injured as I was.

The ride operator, a red-haired teen, loped toward me. "Are you all right, ma'am?" he panted.

I nodded, unable to speak. "I just killed my knee," I admitted to Ellie and Sophie once I found a place to lean.

The next three days were complicated by a knee swollen to twice its normal size. With every step, a sharp pain incited my groans. I limped in two speeds, slow and slower. Would I have exchanged the playful afternoon for a healthy knee? I didn't think so. I had learned to reduce regret by locating the lesson instead. The injury put me on notice. Feel every step of this journey, it told me. Pay attention to every encounter, sense every move. My damaged knee forced my attention, took me out of the fight to the finish, and encouraged me to sit among my family's things to catch my breath. I needed to pay my last respects to evidence now set to join the dust of the ages where no stories are told and no laughter is heard and nobody has to clean up the messes.

The culling from generation to generation had me on a tightrope strung between opposites, the Trash and the Treasure, extremes held together by the thin line of my judgment about what stays and what goes.

The time had come to resuscitate the captives, ridiculous and precious, of Daddy's existence. Trust me when I say that driving through a storage unit entry gate is a feeling like no other. Except maybe driving into a graveyard. The concrete corridors, metal walls, and exposed ceilings were empty of beauty and breath.

In no particular order, Ellie and I sent from the storage unit to the landfill check registers, paystubs, vinyl record collections, embroidered linens, dozens of 2x4s from Grandma's garage, her plastic-wrapped brocade sofa, train sets, war toys, my father's childhood high chair, painted a perfect cherry red, the hardest to let go. In a fit of reasonableness and a drive toward progress, I tagged the high chair for the dump. Ellie's thumbs up meant more to me than the tug in my heart at the thought of baby Leo tasting his first solid food. Her affirmation strengthened my pursuit of reason.

Why hadn't Daddy made us a part of all of this long ago? He had decades to include us in a sensible dismantling of the stuff of three generations. Why not until now? Anger rumbled in my logical core. I wanted to smash the Chinese screen to bits and grind its ivory blossoms to pulp. I wanted to load every last Springfield rifle and Harper's Ferry shotgun onto a raft and capsize the collection in the middle of the Mississippi. I wanted to hack the rugs to ribbons and demolish the model airplanes with a sledgehammer. I wanted to burn the tabletop scrapbooks and photo albums in the dead of night at my father's grave at the national cemetery, a bonfire of gall. But instead I stashed away a child's chamber pot, wrapped porcelain figurines from Japan in Grandma's dish towels, and along with those packed a Persian battle shield, two carved walking sticks, a stained glass window, the wall mirror from my grandfather's barber shop, my grandmother's ironing board and more into the Suburban's back end. All that I rescued, I promised the light of home.

In the final hours of our last day, Ellie and I stood on the catwalk at Public Storage tossing a century of keepings twenty feet below into the open bed of the Junk Genius truck we had hired after we stared each other down as fiercely as we ever had. We agreed that we had no choice. Time had run out. We were forced to dump the remains.

Daddy's history was now shrunken to the measure of memories and artifacts that Ellie and I had decided to keep, that which adhered to our versions of the family story, ones that would last at most another generation, maybe two.

How is it that so much of who we think we are is waylaid, forgotten? We earn membership in the Great Beyond as dismantled selves, galactic fragments dissolved into nomadic particles rejoining the womb of all that is.

Our vehicles stuffed to the gills, Ellie and I crept out of the driveway of the Public Storage on Hunting Valley Road in a final procession for our father. Ellie had Sophie and the load of guns in her van, and I had, among other antiques, the Chinese screen with its decorative and now illegal ivory carvings in mine. I turned on the radio to hear, I kid you not, Gloria Gaynor's "I Will Survive." Once out of the gate, we pulled over to the median for our farewell. As if on cue, a St. Paul police car swerved into the parking lot just as we were getting out of our vehicles. Our hearts jumped, and we did our best to look like the harmless 50-something matrons who we were. We exhaled when he drove on past. An honorary presence? a final salute?

Ellie and I took leave of our vehicles as if custom demanded it.

"We did it, sister," I said, without raising my sunglasses. "Be careful."

"You, too." she replied as we stretched our arms around each other for the last act of what had seemed like an endless journey. Sophie waved from the van as I pulled away.

Who knew when I would return to Minnesota now that Ellie and I had packed up the leftovers to head back to our faraway homes.

As I headed south on I-35, a sudden moment of clarity had me merging onto Highway 5 toward South Minneapolis. I couldn't leave the homeground of my father without one more visit to the Falls. I followed the winding path to the bridge where Sophie had pranced a few days before. My knee had recovered, the pain almost gone. As I stood above the eternal flow that I had come to trust as true and powerful, I considered the odyssey that Ellie and I had begun together when our pyramid of hands traced the distance between North and South on the map that Daddy had unfolded and spread out for us to see. We had been transformed, all of us, by the journey. Who we would have been otherwise didn't matter. "Remember who you ARE," Daddy had declared. A new revision of the verses in Proverbs I had held in my heart since childhood rose to my lips, *"Trust in the flow with all your being, and lean not unto the uncertain self. In every way, acknowledge the Eternal Source and honor its course."*

A gust of wind rustled me back to the day I had been here with Ellie and Daddy on the occasion of his eighty-fifth birthday. I remembered bending to the pile of leaves that played against the stone wall of the overlook, taking a pile into my arms and tossing them into the air, convincing Daddy to do the same. For a moment we were children together, laughing at the pure act of letting go.

part four: restore

she's traveled

to the edge of grace and back,
found lush forests
dripping light,
felt the wet of morning
on wanton pillows,
given a second chance
to almost everything,
watched for rabbits and coyotes,
listened for owls,
hauled water,
acted as the servant
and her queen
and severed any difference,
prayed without ceasing
until she forgot
and forgave
her forgetfulness,
sung with the notes
of creation,
joined by
Knowers of The Way.

forty-five

On the three-day drive across the prairies of Nebraska and westward, I formulated a hypothesis based on all the evidence before me. A blend of *life isn't fair, pay your own way,* and *remember who you are* philosophies guided Daddy's life. Had he washed his hands of the storage units years ago, leaving them for Ellie and me to manage? My questions for Daddy kept growing, but the only place answers might yet appear was in the belongings that intuition had nudged me to keep.

Interstate 80 West traversed the Great Salt Lake Desert, and I anticipated a rest stop at the Bonneville Salt Flats, a stretch of blinding white that Trish, Mocha, and I had seen together over the course of our move to California what seemed an infinity ago.

Ready for a break after two hours of driving, I stretched upright and took several deep breaths. The reflective terrain that had once played host to a space capsule landing[61] pulled me to venture away from the traffic noise, the parked cars, the mundane repetitions that define rest stops. I walked onto the mineralized crust far enough to feel insignificant. There I stood, squinting at the power of evaporation. I thought about the life I had been born into: my family history, the subterranean racism of my youth, the biblical indoctrination, the ways out (trial and error, travel, creative effort, friendship, nature), my many questions, injuries both given and received, the instinct to remove what is not needed in order to thrive. My spark of awareness conjured an inner whirlwind of all the paradises and purgatories that had moved me to this moment, including my life with Daddy, Momma, and Ellie. We all had a hand in each other's losses, but we also had a hand

---

[61] In 2004, the *Stardust* spacecraft released its sample-return capsule for a landing in the Bonneville Salt Flats after its flybys of asteroid 5535 Annefrank in 2002 and comet Wild 2 in 2004.

in each other's dreams. One did not exist without the other in a world that wasn't fair but told the truth. I was left to make what I would of my story. On that bright sheet of salted desert, I asked forgiveness for everything I had ever done to cause them and anyone else harm. In the dry glare, my tears vanished before they fell.

forty-six

A visitation of spirits circled the possessions I hauled the many miles to my California home. What odd foragers were those who had preceded me. What great truths were buried in the stuff of their lives? What revelations awaited?

The experiences of the past year were still rocketing my credit card balance and cluttering tabletops and image galleries with pickings meant to jog my memory about something meaningful. What design was intended, and how might it map my purpose as life became less about cleaning up someone else's business and more about tending mine?

"I have no idea where to begin!" I confessed to Trish in a quiet morning moment.

"Start where you are," she counseled, calling to mind the wisdom of Pema Chodron, a valued spiritual teacher of mine.

"You're funny." I raised my coffee mug in a toasting gesture and noted the message painted on its surface: *Bloom Where You Are Planted*. Trish and I had been using the same mugs for the five years since our life had shoved us onto an obstacle course. I had splurged on the original ceramic art pieces from our favorite coffeehouse in Colorado. Trish's read *Be Someone Who Makes You Happy*. The mugs hung from their own special dragonfly hooks above the kitchen sink and were the vessels for our coffee ritual. I gave her advice a second thought. "Maybe you're right. Thanks, honey."

I slouched into my workspace, a room painted turquoise by Trish's own generous hands. She knew I loved the colors of the southwest, so she painted the room during one of my visits to St. Paul. I came home to a grand surprise. In that cheery space, I set up my grandmother's ironing board as a standing desk and had piles of papers, files, and envelopes still to go through from Daddy's collections. I thought about how I used to open my red leather Bible and point without looking, finding a verse that could serve as a talisman for the moment. Just pick up something, I told myself. Anything. What had Trish said? *Start where you are!*

I shuffled around one of the smaller stacks and pulled out a yellowing newspaper folded over itself. I opened it to read the bold, block print from the April 5, 1968 edition of *The Commercial Appeal*, the Memphis newspaper that was delivered to our driveway in Clarksdale every morning: DR. KING IS SLAIN BY SNIPER. Daddy! Point for you! Whatever his motivation for keeping the headline, I was proud to hold such a piece of history in my hands.

Another item slipped from its folds. The newspaper cradled an unsealed envelope that held pages from a legal pad, the kind Dad would have taken on surveillance and to interviews, holding notes that would inform official reports.

The papers unfolded to reveal his handwriting printed in what looked like government-issue blue ink. A four-page poem followed, scathing couplets, bitter rhymes, the evidence, untitled, undated, unsigned. "Trish, come here!" I hollered. "I have to show you something.'

She rounded the corner and Mocha's nails tip-tapped behind her. I made a brief explanation, then asked her if I could read the poem aloud.

"Of course, you can. You must!" Her support of me had not waivered over this long slog of sense-making.

"Here goes." I began, my voice wary to give rise to words under wraps for so long.

> "I can't wait to get out of this state, where murder
> and beatings are legal and great....

My shock at the words returned at the same time my gut felt the internal beat of the lines. Keep reading, I told myself.

> "Where kluckers and coofers are vying for cheers
> And the natives all say, 'There's nothing wrong here.
> Freedom Now! Keep the white race white!
> Let's burn a church on Sunday night!...

I stole a look at Trish while I came up for air. She stared at me, dumbfounded.

> ...Yessir, we treat 'em all right—Beat 'em in jail late at night.
> Lend 'em money if we can and give 'em "furnish" beyond that
> to keep 'em toiling for a shack on a hill out of the shade
> where you can see they have it made....'
> ...No room for progress or utopia for all,
> So, I can't wait. Goodbye, y'all."

My voice trembled at the end. I cleared my throat of the hot sarcasm of Daddy's words, but they steamed the air. My deepest loss had been the feeling that I never saw to the bottom of my father's soul. Here was a glimmer of a man who observed the same ugliness I had seen in my youth and felt similar disgust. His long-standing self-suppression gave me a strange and harsh comfort.

What luck had rescued this rhythmic confession from the wreckage? Where had I found the prize? During the basement raids during those nights when Daddy was in ICU? In the storage units as I made random assessments on the value of things, maybe when I was resting my knee, digging through a box in the dim light of late afternoon, the flashlight going weak? Had I seen the yellowed newsprint and assumed importance? I couldn't recall. I thought back to how exhausted I had been for all that emptying and could only claim divine intervention.

I imagined Daddy in his younger days, wearing a white-starched shirt and his skinny black tie, his G-man look, standing on the Baptist church lawn across from our house in Clarksdale, a megaphone in his hand, reciting his words in the shadow of the steeple, detailing his cynical views for the neighborhood. *Thanks for the evidence, Daddy*, I whispered as I slipped the precious pages back into the folds of the newspaper.

The next day, I picked up a text from Ellie. "No news from the dealer," it read. We discovered in our research that our grandfather's personal gun collection once had been the most extensive in the region, according to a 1957 article in the *Minneapolis Star-Tribune*. As executor, Ellie was looking to sell the lot except for a few kept for the grandchildren. I wrote to her that I didn't want any guns. I had seen little good come from them. Then, I remembered that she had shown me a hardscrabble gun pounded out by a blacksmith that had been used by a slave heading for freedom on the Underground Railroad. It had been a gift to my grandfather, an object of hope and courage. I wanted that one, I told her. But I didn't say a word about Daddy's poem. That secret was mine for now.

I said goodbye to Daddy during a massage, at the tail end when all was like jelly and the violet of the crown chakra pulsed behind my eyes. My neck had been loosened, my shoulders unfettered, energies balanced and settled by a body healer with decades of practice. How stubborn I had become, so rigid and sure that I knew best how to hold myself together. It took a while for me to remember how to let go, how to relax at the tap of a thumb or the pressure of a palm or the tips of fingers. Jewel taught me again and again. "Feel that? That's you resisting." The body doesn't lie. And it can be stubborn to change. She worked and worked, and even with my consciousness engaged, a fervor kept my muscles at attention. I urged leniency, release, and though the process was slow, helped with Jewel's patience, an eventual loosening wiggled into play.

At times, I felt the dance between Jewel's hands and my muscled skeleton. Near the end of the session, she placed her warm hand behind my neck and held it there like a parent would a newborn. Time traveled backward. I imagined myself in my parents' arms, the way they must have held with love and wonder the infant named Sharon Hope. A spiraling tunnel devoid of fear appeared behind my closed eyelids. I thought of the funeral and how I had centered the boy Daddy had been behind the waterfall safe in a place of childhood wonder. It was time to set him free. *Be on your way, Daddy. May your stardust travel to destinations unknown, to other worlds needing the dose of a good guy, an explorer, a law keeper, a father who loved his daughters in the best ways he knew how, leaving so many tracks to help me circle toward home.*

forty-seven

Christmas Day began with a bang. Trish and I had just taken our first sips of coffee in the dim light of morning to a jazzy version of "Home for the Holidays" when THUNK! CRASH! CLATTER! We sent each other jolted looks.

"What in the world?" I shouted as barking took over.

"It's okay, girl," Trish reassured Mocha as I stood to investigate.

Immediately I saw nothing but blank space where a decorative glass bowl had hung, its straw macrame hanger now dangled empty. I had suspended the globe near other family treasures found in the storage units: the mirror from my great-grandfather's barber shop, the stool from my grandfather's workbench, the pitcher from my great grandmother's washbowl, Grandma Sig's barrister bookshelves, a magnetism of objects from Daddy's family tree. The faux fishbowl, a solid three pounds of golden, crackled glass, displayed painted fish floating across its sparkling surface. I knew little of the fishbowl, its history already forgotten. The vessel was useless but for its beauty.

I scuttled over to assess the damage and collected the largest piece, a full half still intact. An image pinged of the apple half I had placed on the altar when I parted with my vocation. I placed the smaller pieces one by one into the jagged hollow that remained. An experience from a recent mosaics class flashed into my mind. Could I reimagine the pieces? Into what? A gazing ball for the garden? I would bag the broken contents, put them away for a while, and in time create something new. Then, I remembered something Patrice had told me in the months before, "Watch for visitations. He'll come. Pay attention."

I looked again at the frayed straw as the last measures of the song floated into silence. Something nudged me to speak to the emptiness. "Daddy? Was that you?"

epilogue

Under the blue, the ginko pranced in place, its saucy green leaves popping. Bees nestled in the lavender, and the young Japanese maple's red-tipped shoots flaunted their youth at every puff of air. The wind chime Ellie had given me in honor of Daddy tingled in the sway of the delta breeze. Mocha sat like a sphynx on the cushiest grass in the backyard near the blue juniper I had planted and named Daddy's Tree. Trish was in the kitchen concocting a curry when I called to her, "Geese!" We met at the back steps and gazed upward at the exodus. I took Trish's hand, and she squeezed mine in return. What were we if not believers in change and migration?

Epistle of **HOPE,** *continued*

[13]Certain stories kept circling, every retelling offering new questions, fresh takes, chances to find humor where it hadn't been, dares to be truer in reflection. [14]Writing strengthened the spine, gave the posture needed to look straight into the eyes of what was. [15]The rambles of time leaked into the pages kept, memories like birds, returning again from great distances, heavensent reminders that questions themselves were sublime. [16]She could trust the compendium of all that had been breathed and felt and known. [17]An eternal truth echoed from the well of time: everything is home.

∞

acknowledgments

This memoir did not materialize as a solo effort. I was born into the world with guides at every corner offering ways to go, supplying a sense of direction. To the cartographers and sages I honor in these lines, I say thank you. To those not named, I also say thank you. Each of you represents a unique figure in a fantastic array of archetypes on this pilgrim's journey, all of you alert to the call for help when it arrived, some just yesterday, some decades past. I befriended you as members of my pack, all lovers of the world, all true to who you determined yourselves to be and supportive of the universal right to own one's story.

To my Southern muses, Eudora, Flannery, and Harper; to Nola; to school teachers, Mrs. Hubbard, Mrs. Bounds, Miss Butler, Miss Strode, and Ms. Troutman; to all the music and news that came through my transisor radio; to spiritual mentors Pema, Parker, Richard, and Tara; to my 1990s Rice University School Writing Project fellows, to my Courage and Renewal Circles of Trust, to my patient, insightful first readers to my writing mentors, to the courageous Sacramento women writers at Women's Wisdom Art and Sisters of the Pen; to my Houston peeps and allies to my Colorado compadres to soul sister Patricia E.; to book coach and designer, Heather; to change-agent nonprofits Center for Action and Contemplation, Mississippi Civil Rights Museum, The Houston Holocaust Museum, The National Museum of Women in the Arts, Peer Spirit, The Southern Poverty Law Center, The School of Lost Borders, The United States Memorial Holocaust Museum, and Women's Wisdom Art; to the Sacramento Public Library, the Clarksdale Public Library, the Tyler Public Library, and libraries and their librarians everywhere; and most importantly, to my mother, sister, children, my beloved, and to those who first guided me to unimagined worlds: Debra, Anne, Janet, and Daddy.

I toast you, generous ones, for seasoning the layered truth that has been born in my story. May all that is holy inhabit your hearts and may all that is good direct your desires.

In ever deepening gratitude, Sharon

I also thank the research sources that provided reputable details and commentary helpful in presenting the historical and sociological information that I include.

Hancock, Lee. "Robert E. Lee High School, Race, and Segregation in Tyler: A 130-Year Timeline." The Tyler Loop , 1 Sept. 2017, https://thetylerloop.com/robert-e-lee-high-school-race-and-segregation-in-tyler-a-130-year-timeline/ .

Hamlin, Françoise N. Crossroads at Clarksdale: The Black Freedom Struggle in the Mississippi Delta After World War II . University of North Carolina Press, 2012.

National Association of Black Journalists (NABJ), which states that "whenever a color is used to appropriately describe race then it should be capitalized, including White and Brown."

history.com, pbs.com, native-land.ca

about the author

Sharon is the great-grand-daughter of Swedish and Norwegian immigrants who settled in Wisconsin, Minnesota, and Illinois. Her father's F.B.I. career took her family South during the 1960s. She lived most of her adulthood there, devoting herself to her children and her teaching career. Since her girlhood, Sharon has used writing as a conduit for self-awareness, creative expression, and connection to others. She relies on her powers of observation and contemplation to orient herself toward equity, justice, and kindness. Sharon's prose and poetry have appeared in a variety of publications. She resides in California with her beloved and their two dogs. Find her blog and resources for renewal at sharonhopefabriz.com.

www.ingramcontent.com/pod-product-compliance
Lightning Source LLC
Chambersburg PA
CBHW031106080526
44587CB00011B/855